*Start Your Own*

# PERSONAL TRAINING BUSINESS

# Additional titles in *Entrepreneur's* **Startup Series**

## *Start Your Own*

**Entrepreneur**
MAGAZINE'S

# start*up*

**2ND EDITION**

## *Start Your Own*

# PERSONAL TRAINING BUSINESS

*Your Step-by-Step
Guide to Success*

*Entrepreneur Press and Tom Weede*

**EP**
Entrepreneur.
Press

Editorial Director: Jere L. Calmes
Managing Editor: Marla Markman
Cover Design: Beth Hansen-Winter
Production and Composition: Eliot House Productions

This publication is designed to provide accurate and authoritative information in regard to the subject matter covered. It is sold with the understanding that the publisher is not engaged in rendering legal, accounting or other professional services. If legal advice or other expert assistance is required, the services of a competent professional person should be sought.

**Library of Congress Cataloging-in-Publication Data**
Weede, Tom.
    Start your own personal training business/by Entrepreneur Press and Tom Weede.—2nd ed.
        p.    cm.    —(Start your own series)
    Includes index.
    ISBN-10: 1-59918-148-7 (alk. paper)
    ISBN-13: 978-1-59918-148-6
        1. Personal trainers—Handbooks, manuals, etc. 2. Personal trainers—Vocational guidance. 3. Personal trainers—Finance, Personal. 4. Physical fitness centers—Management—Handbooks, manuals, etc. I. Weede, Tom. II. Entrepreneur Press.
    GV428.7.S83 2007
    338.7'616137—dc22                                        2007030576

Printed in the United States of America

# Contents

# Preface

Almost every day, it seems, there is a major story in the popular media that focuses on health and fitness. From breakthrough nutrition research, to tips on starting a walking program, to advice on improving flexibility, the coverage reaches literally millions of people through newspapers, magazines, books, web sites, and television shows.

And yet, the same popular media frequently reports about the obesity problem. The familiar numbers are heard so often that the shock value is wearing off: About a third of U.S. adults are considered obese, while another third are considered overweight. All told, those statistics encompass a population of more than 133 million people.

It's a great paradox—with all we know about healthy living, why are many people still struggling to get in shape?

Maybe there is just too much information and people are overwhelmed. Or perhaps they lack the motivation necessary to carry through on a fitness program. Whatever the reason, as a personal trainer you have both a great opportunity and a significant challenge. You are in demand to help people not just wade through all of the information, but to inspire them to apply it and improve their lives.

As a result, starting a personal training business offers a satisfying combination of financial reward and a career in which you can make a profound difference in the lives of others. A skilled trainer who also has good business knowledge and judgment can earn a substantial income.

At the same time, because many people still face troubling weight and healthy lifestyle issues, new approaches are needed if fitness professionals are to reach these individuals.

Fortunately, the fitness business is rising to the challenge by creating innovative ways to do just that. And this means that you have new avenues to entrepreneurial success through strategies that will grow your business by making fitness relevant and accessible for more and more people.

So in this updated second edition, we've given you information that will quickly get you up to speed on these exciting directions in the fitness industry, and show you how you can take advantage of them. You'll see, for example, how the emerging field of wellness coaching is using important discoveries in behavior modification to access the powerful internal motivations of clients. Also, we cover how trainers are eschewing a one-size-fits-all approach and targeting their training services toward the specific needs of particular populations, such as youth or older adults. We explain how fitness organizations also are responding by offering specialized certifications or continuing education that better prepare trainers to address the needs of particular segments of clients.

What's more, we describe how functional training is being used to help sedentary clients better perform the tasks of everyday living. A personal trainer today must be well-versed in the theories behind functional training—trust us, your competitors will be. And, more importantly, trainers must know how to put theory into practice and deliver effective and safe functional workouts to clients.

This second edition also includes expanded information on how the internet can revolutionize your business. Having a web site is almost mandatory, and will give you instant credibility, no matter what the size of your company. We explain how you can bring your business into cyberspace, either by creating a simple web site that acts as an electronic brochure for your training business, or by setting up a site that allows you to train clients online.

As with the first edition, this book generally focuses on the business side of personal training. This is not an instruction book on training technique—there are plenty of certification and education programs where you can find that.

But we realize that you're interested in exercise, athletic performance and how science is exploring ways that we can become fitter and healthier. You wouldn't be a personal trainer or a soon-to-be trainer if you weren't. So we've added sidebars throughout the book giving you "Research Insights"—you'll find these fascinating, we're sure. But they're also perfect tidbits of information that you can pass along to your clients to enhance your reputation as a reliable source of health and fitness knowledge.

And this book, of course, also covers the nitty gritty details of starting and running a successful fitness business. Whether you're looking to launch a solo concern with minimal investment or to open your own studio and hire other trainers, this book will help you. You'll get an overview of the industry and potential client markets, as well as a step-by-step guide to setting up and operating your fitness business. You'll learn about start-up costs, marketing, and how to track and manage your company's finances. Successful personal trainers and industry experts will share the insights they've gained through years of experience.

Regardless of the type of personal training business you want to start, we recommend that you read every chapter in this book. Most of the information applies to all sizes and types of personal training operations, and the information is interrelated.

Good luck as you embark on a business venture that will not only challenge and invigorate you professionally and personally, but also vastly improve the lives of your clients.

# 1

# Introduction to
# Personal Training

This is an exciting time to be an entrepreneurial personal trainer. The opportunities for qualified fitness professionals who also understand how to run a business are virtually unlimited.

Take a look around. Obesity is an epidemic. Many people of all ages are spending too much time in front of computers and televisions, and this increasingly sedentary lifestyle is taking a tremendous toll on their health. Fast food restaurants serve up calorie-dense meals and regular restaurants offer massive portion sizes.

As people decide to do something about their expanding waistlines and finally get in shape, fitness professionals are well-positioned to help. Whether it's baby boomers wanting to regain some of their youthful vitality or parents looking for ways to provide positive role models for their children, they are turning to trainers. As well, doctors and managed care organizations have recognized that diet and exercise are an important part of keeping people healthy and avoiding unnecessary health-care costs. Even companies are realizing that healthy, fit employees are more productive.

So it's no surprise that personal training is one of the top professions of the 21st century and a fast-growing segment of the fitness industry. With rare exceptions, personal trainers love what they do. After all, they're not working on a production line or sitting in front of a computer—they're helping people get and stay healthy and fit. And for their efforts, they're earning $40 to $150 or more per hour.

"The industry is continuing to grow," says Tony Ordas, former director of certification for the American Council on Exercise (ACE). "There has been a steady increase in growth in the number of health and fitness facilities. More and more clubs are in dire need of personal trainers." While some of those clubs want their trainers to work as employees, many others are hiring independent contractors or contracting with personal training companies to meet their needs—and that means opportunity for you.

Just how many health clubs are there nationwide? According to information from the International Health, Racquet, and Sportsclub Association (IHRSA), as of January 2007, there were more than 29,000 U.S. health clubs and 42.7 million health club members. There was a total of $17.6 billion in health club industry revenue in 2006, reports IHRSA.

# What Do Personal Trainers Do?

Personal trainers work with clients who need instruction and coaching in the areas of exercise physiology, kinesiology, nutrition, supplementation, fitness assessment, exercise programming, sports conditioning, flexibility techniques, and more. More often they train with individuals one-on-one, but sometimes also train couples and small groups.

Typically, personal trainers begin their work with a particular client by doing an assessment. Through conversation and by completing forms, they gather information about the client's health and medical status, lifestyle, expectations, and preferences.

Then they are able to establish realistic and measurable short- and long-term goals and develop an exercise program.

As they work with each client, personal trainers teach safe and effective exercise techniques; they monitor, record, and evaluate progress; they make adjustments in the program as necessary; and they provide support and motivation to help their clients stick to the program and reach their goals. Personal trainers may also serve as consultants when their clients are setting up training equipment in their homes or offices.

Personal trainers who have studied nutrition may also offer nutrition and weight management counseling. Trainers who are group fitness instructors may incorporate popular group fitness trends into small group training sessions. For example, your clients may not want to participate in a crowded class at the gym but may want you to lead very small classes in areas such as yoga, kickboxing, and body sculpting for themselves, their families, and friends.

## Every Stripe and Shape

**S**o what do personal trainers really do? Some of the services typically offered by personal trainers include:

- ○ Fitness assessments
- ○ Individual exercise programs
- ○ Individual weight/fat-loss programs
- ○ Nutrition consulting
- ○ Strength and endurance training
- ○ In-home or in-office personal training
- ○ Personal training for teenagers and children
- ○ Personal training for seniors
- ○ Sports conditioning
- ○ Wellness coaching
- ○ Stress management programs
- ○ Cardio respiratory programs
- ○ Flexibility exercises
- ○ Individually designed high- or low-impact step and aerobics programs
- ○ Individual or small group training
- ○ Seminars and classes on fitness

# Research Insight

**J**ust how many calories your client burns during exercise depends on a number of factors, including how much muscle mass they're using. For example, because of the upper-body involvement, running burns more calories than biking. Also, weight-bearing activities expend more calories than weight-supported pursuits—so your client will spend more calories running than swimming. According to a 2000 compendium in *Medicine and Science in Sport and Exercise*, a 180-pound person will burn (per hour) 1,023 calories running at an 8 minute per mile pace, 982 calories cycling at 16 to 19 mile per hour, and 818 calories swimming vigorously.

Some personal trainers work with people who have suffered an illness or injury and need assistance transitioning back to a physically active lifestyle. This is an area known as "clinical exercise" and is an important part of the rehabilitation process. Trainers work in conjunction with their clients' medical doctors and physical therapists to establish an appropriate exercise program; then they instruct the client as necessary to implement the program.

Trainers work with amateur and professional athletes to help them maintain their conditioning during their off-season and be prepared for in-season competition. They work with performers who may or may not be celebrities, but who need to stay in top physical form.

Jennifer Brilliant's Brooklyn-based company offers one-on-one training, as well as group training in exercise and yoga. Jennifer and her trainers work in homes, offices, schools, and gyms.

Lynne Wells, in New York City, works with clients in their homes and in the gyms located in residential buildings where the clients live.

Bill Sonnemaker owns Catalyst Fitness in the Atlanta area, and employs three full-time trainers and two part-time trainers. He's the recipient of the 2007 IDEA International Personal Trainer of the Year Award and the 2007 National Academy of Sports Medicine Pursuit of Excellence in Health and Fitness Award. One of the keys to his success, he says, is his time as an

## Stat Fact

According to a report from the U.S. Surgeon General's office, 60 percent of American adults exercise only once in a while and 25 percent never exercise.

intern and employee of other trainers. "I had access to good coaches with good exercise technique, and learned proper form and proper program design," he says.

Personal trainers are not simply exercise instructors and supervisors—in other words, there's more to being a personal trainer than just knowing your anatomy and exercise physiology and the sciences behind exercise. Trainers are confidants, role models, and sources of support and encouragement. And when you have a business offering personal training services, you'll do even more than that—handling everything from marketing to selling to accounting to employee relations.

# Who Is Your Market?

Successful personal trainers agree that there is no such thing as a "typical" client. More and more people, regardless of their level of fitness or exercise expertise, are turning to personal trainers as a practical and affordable means of becoming and staying healthy. Hard-core strength trainers and body builders are only part of the overall clientele of personal trainers.

Jennifer B.'s clients include businesspeople, stay-at-home mothers, and people recovering from injuries and illnesses. "Some people are striving to get into better shape, whatever that means for them," she says. "Some are into maintenance, so they're not really trying to improve, they just want to stay where they are. Some people want to learn something new for variety."

How long do clients typically stay with a personal trainer? It can range from just a few sessions to years. Some trainers carefully seek out long-term clients; others choose a niche where they educate a client about fitness, or work them through a short-term problem, then move on. Jennifer says her clients stay with her an average of three to five years.

Some clients want frequent sessions with their trainers, as many as two and three a week. Others opt to see their trainers less often, perhaps just to do periodic fitness testing, measure their progress, and update their program. Lynne W. says she typically sees her clients one to three times a week, and most have been with her for more than three years.

Realize that not everyone who has an interest in fitness is a potential client; many dedicated fitness buffs prefer to do their own thing. Along the same line, not everyone who needs a personal trainer is going to be willing and/or able to hire one.

# Is This Business for You?

There are two key aspects to owning a personal training business. The first is being a personal trainer, and the second is being an entrepreneur.

Good personal trainers are passionate about fitness and eager to learn the latest information about exercise, nutrition, and healthy lifestyles. They enjoy helping and teaching others about fitness and exercise. They are caring, giving, patient, and empathetic. They absolutely love the idea of spending ten hours per day working with people in a gym or other setting, guiding them through exercises, and helping them reach their fitness goals.

> **Bright Idea**
>
> If you're not sure how you'll do at running a personal training business, try working as an independent contractor first. You'll get a taste of being self-employed and can decide from there if you want to go further.

As a trainer, your job is to motivate your clients, improve their techniques, and keep their workouts fun and effective. You need to be friendly, enthusiastic, and have great communication skills to do this. It also helps to be personable, genuine, and truly sincere—you're not trying to sell anything; you're helping people, and for that, you get paid.

Successful entrepreneurs have the ability to step beyond doing the service their company offers and deal with the process of building and running a business. To own your own personal training business, you'll need strong management, administrative, and marketing skills—or you'll need to recognize what you don't have and then cultivate them in yourself or be willing to hire people who can provide those skills.

As Bill S. says, "Being good at your job as a trainer is completely different than being a good marketer or good business owner . . . So finding your strengths and weaknesses is important."

Jennifer B. was a dancer for many years before she became a personal trainer. For her, the appeal of personal training was "sharing and helping others." Jennifer says, "It's a profession where people are giving, and with that generosity, people are successful." But she knows she has to do more than just work with clients. "The part of the business that's challenging is the day-to-day things you have to do, all the details of running a business—the bookkeeping, handling phone calls, keeping records straight," she says. "It's surprising how much time running the business takes."

# Credibility and Credentials

There are no professional licensing requirements for personal trainers. That means anyone can call himself a personal trainer and open up a business. But consumers are becoming increasingly savvy, and most will ask about your credentials before they hire you. That's why certifications and professional affiliations are critical.

## Smart Tip

*Tip...*

Even though certification is not required at present, it's always possible that legislation requiring some sort of licensure or certification could be passed in any state at anytime. If that happens and you're not certified, you're out of business. So get certified. And insist that the trainers who work for you be certified as well.

"The big difference between licensure and certification is that certification is voluntary, whereas licensure is mandated by the state," says Ordas. "Certification is a credential that states you have a certain level of knowledge and skill."

There may be more than 300 organizations offering certification programs—some general, others very specialized—for personal trainers (although it doesn't appear that anyone keeps an official count). Most are for-profit, but a few are nonprofit. The majority of these organizations also offer education programs leading to certification, although several merely administer tests to determine competency. Some of the education and certification organizations also function like a professional association, providing individuals who have

# It's Official!

**S**ome of the certifications you might want to consider obtaining include:

- ◯ Aerobic Fitness Trainer
- ◯ Aqua Fitness Specialist
- ◯ Certified Fitness Advisor
- ◯ Certified Personal Trainer
- ◯ Clinical Exercise Specialist
- ◯ First Responder/First Aid
- ◯ Fitness Therapist
- ◯ Golf Fitness Trainer
- ◯ Group Fitness Instructor
- ◯ Health Fitness Instructor
- ◯ Lifestyle and Weight Management Consultant
- ◯ Neonatal/Postpartum Exercise Specialist
- ◯ Wellness Coach
- ◯ Performance Nutrition Specialist
- ◯ Personal Defense Specialist
- ◯ Rehabilitation Exercise Specialist
- ◯ Senior Fitness Specialist
- ◯ Specialist in Fitness for the Physically Limited
- ◯ Specialist in Martial Art Conditioning
- ◯ Sports Conditioning Specialist
- ◯ Strength and Conditioning Specialist
- ◯ Water Fitness Trainer
- ◯ Youth Fitness Trainer

completed their programs with a range of ongoing support services. And then there are professional associations, which are just that—an association of personal trainers and other fitness professionals. A number of these organizations are listed in the Appendix; you can find even more by doing a search on the internet or visiting your local library.

With such an abundance of choices, it makes sense to recognize that you can't belong to every fitness organization out there. That's an expensive and counterproductive approach. Study the organizations and choose the one(s) that meet your requirements and will give you the tools you need to succeed.

When deciding on the organization(s) you'll work with to obtain your credentials, consider these issues:

- *Accreditation.* Check to see if the certifying organization is accredited, and by whom. It's a good idea to also check into the accreditation agency to determine how they set standards and what sort of reputation they have. Although there are hundreds of personal training certification organizations, only a handful of nationally recognized organizations are accredited by the National Commission for Certifying Agencies. This is the accreditation body of National Organization for Competency Assurance, which sets quality standards for credentialing organizations.

- *Club requirements.* If you are going to contract with a club or spa to provide their personal training services, they may require that you and the trainers on your staff be certified through specific organizations. Find out what they prefer before investing in a program they won't accept.

- *Your goals.* Be sure the certification is something you can use and is in line with the goals and aspirations you have for yourself and your company.

- *Your market.* The certification should be appropriate for the market segment you want to serve.

- *Your educational needs.* Some certifying organizations offer only testing programs that determine skills and competency; others offer training programs that lead to certification. Your own needs will determine which you choose. For more information on how to evaluate a certification organization, see Chapter 8.

Beyond industry-related certification, many personal trainers have college degrees in health/exercise sciences or related fields. These degrees demonstrate your knowledge and commitment to the field.

A sampling of some of the trainers we interviewed reveals the value they place on maintaining qualifications. In addition to two certifications from the American Council on Exercise (ACE), Jennifer B. also holds a fine arts degree in dance. Bill S.'s credentials include work as a research chemist for the Centers for Disease Control and Prevention, a pending master's degree in exercise science, and certifications through the

## Dollar Stretcher

If you live near a medical school, take advantage of their medical libraries, which contain textbooks and journals that are more expensive to buy or subscribe to than most personal trainers can afford. These are your best sources for timely, accurate information. You should also check out www.pubmed.com, which allows you to search academic journals based on key words—abstracts are free, and many journals are now making full-text articles free, as well (some require a delay of up to a year after publication before giving free access).

National Academy of Sports Medicine, the National Strength and Conditioning Association, the American College of Sports Medicine (ACSM), and ACE. Lynne W. is certified through ACE, has a certification in Lifestyle and Weight Management Consulting, and two certifications in Hatha yoga. Richard Cotton holds a certification through ACSM, as well as a master's degree in physical education with an emphasis in applied exercise science. If you choose to pursue a degree, Richard says, "physical education, kinesiology, and exercise physiology (all with an applied emphasis as opposed to research emphasis)" are helpful courses of study for this field.

## Continuing Education

Once you receive a certification, the organization will likely require you to earn continuing education units (CEUs) on a periodic basis to maintain that credential. Most offer a wide range of classes and seminars for a fee, so it's easy to choose sessions that are of interest and appropriate for your particular operation. Before signing up for a class, be sure to confirm how many CEUs you'll earn and what sort of documentation is required to be sure you get proper credit.

## Sound Off on Your Certifications

Atlanta-based Bill S. requires each of his trainers to eventually obtain certifications from four of the top organizations: the National Academy of Sports Medicine, the American College of Sports Medicine, the American Council on Exercise, and the National Strength and Conditioning Association. "All of our trainers have at least two of those to begin to work with clients," he says. "This requirement is just so far above any other facility that we advertise on that."

Whether it's required or not, you should always be educating yourself on the latest trends and discoveries in the fitness industry. New products and techniques are constantly being introduced, and you should be familiar with them so you know when to use them with your clients. In fact, a great place to take seminars is at the various trade shows and conventions where equipment vendors are displaying their products. Also, your clients may hear about various fitness-related issues in the consumer media, and you need to be prepared to answer their questions with confidence and accuracy.

Remember that your certifications and the continuing education necessary to maintain them underpin your business success. "The knowledge I've obtained while preparing for certification exams," Bill. S. says, "as well the teaching and education required to maintain those certifications, has made me a better trainer when it comes to assessments, program design, and psychological factors in dealing with clients."

# Designing Your
# Business

Some entrepreneurs would rather walk on hot coals than sit down and write a business plan. Other would-be business owners get so caught up in planning every detail that they never get their businesses off the ground. You need to find a happy medium between these two extremes.

▲

Your personal training company should start with a written business plan. Writing your plan down forces you to think it through and gives you a chance to examine it for consistency and thoroughness. Whether you've got years of personal training experience behind you, or you're brand new to the industry, you need a plan for your business.

This chapter will focus on a few issues particular to planning personal training businesses, but they are by no means all you need to consider when writing your plan.

If you're excited about your business, creating a business plan should be an exciting process. It will help you define and evaluate the overall feasibility of your concept, clarify your goals, and determine what you'll need for start-up and long-term operations.

This is a living, breathing document that will provide you with a road map for your company. You'll use it as a guide, referring to it regularly as you work through the start-up process and during the ongoing operation of your business. And if you're going to be seeking outside financing, either in the form of loans or investors, your business plan will be the tool that convinces funding sources of your venture's worth.

Putting together a business plan is not a linear process, although the final product may look that way. As you work through it, you'll likely find yourself jumping from equipment requirements to cash flow forecasts to staffing, then back to cash flow, on to marketing, and back to equipment requirements. Take your time developing your plan. Whether you want to start a part-time business as a trainer going to clients' homes or establish a fully equipped studio, you're making a serious commitment, and you shouldn't rush into it.

# Business Plan Elements

Though the specific content of your business plan will be unique, there is a basic format that you should follow. This will ensure that you address all the issues you need to, as well as provide lenders and investors with a document to evaluate that is organized in a familiar way. The basic elements are:

- *Front matter.* This includes your cover page, a table of contents, and a statement of purpose.
- *Business description.* Describe the specific personal training business you intend to start and list the reasons you can make it successful. This section should also include your business philosophy, goals, industry analysis, operations, inventory, and start-up timetable.
- *Marketing plan.* Include an overview of the market, a description of your potential customers, a discussion of the advantages and drawbacks of your location, an analysis of the competition, and how you plan to promote your specific business.

- *Company organization.* Describe your management structure, your staffing needs and how you expect to meet them, the consultants and advisors who will be assisting you, your legal structure, and the certifications, licenses, permits, and other regulatory issues that will affect your operations.

- *Financial data.* This is where you show the source(s) of your start-up capital and how you're going to use the money. Include information on real estate, fixtures, equipment, and insurance. You'll also include your financial statements: balance sheet, profit-and-loss statement, break-even analysis, personal financial statements, and personal federal income tax returns.

**Bright Idea**

Your business plan should include worst-case scenarios, both for your own benefit and for your funding sources. You'll benefit from thinking ahead about what you'll do if things don't go the way you want them to. You'll also increase the comfort level of your lenders/investors by demonstrating your ability to deal with adversity and potentially negative situations.

- *Financial projections.* Take your financial data and project it out to show what your business will do. Include projected income statements for three to five years, cash flow statements for three to five years, along with worst-case scenario income and cash flow statements to show what you'll do if your plan doesn't work. Keep in mind that if you're opening a studio, it typically will take until your second year to turn a profit. And when you take into account paying back your investors, it may take until the third year before you have positive cash flow, says Steve Tharrett, president of Club Industry Consulting, a Dallas-based fitness and sports industry consulting company. "Some type of negative cash flow is going to occur at the beginning," he says. "It's really rare that you'll ever make a profit your first year."

- *Summary.* Bring your plan together in this section. If you're trying to appeal to a funding source, use this section to reiterate the merits of your plan.

- *Appendices.* Use this for supporting documents, such as your facility design and layout, marketing studies, sample advertising, copies of leases, and licensing information.

# To Market, to Market

Market research provides businesses with data that allows them to identify and reach particular market segments, and to solve or avoid marketing problems. A

## Smart Tip

When you think your plan is complete, look at it with a fresh eye. Is it realistic? Does it take into account all the possible variables that could affect your operation? After you're satisfied, ask two or three professional associates you trust to evaluate your plan. Use their input to correct any problems before you invest time and money.

thorough market survey forms the foundation of any successful business. It would be impossible to develop marketing strategies or an effective product line without market research.

The goal of market research is for you to identify your market, find out where it is, and develop a strategy to communicate with prospective customers in a way that will convince them to buy from you. Market research will also give you information you need about your competitors. It's important for you to know what they're doing and how that meets—or doesn't meet—the needs of the market.

Marketing consultant Debbie LaChusa, of 10stepmarketing in Santee, California, suggests checking with the major certifying organizations such as the American Council on Exercise (ACE) or the American College of Sports Medicine (ACSM) to find out how many certified trainers they have in your area. "This will give you an idea of the competition," she says. "Also ask if these organizations can provide any information about the specialties these trainers have, such as older adult fitness."

You'll also want to find out how many gyms, health clubs, and exercise studios are in your geographic service area. This speaks to both competition and opportunity. A simple browse through the Yellow Pages will tell you what you need to know. "Talk to some of the clubs and trainers to gauge how business is," LaChusa advises. "Is it weak? Strong? More than they can handle?"

Study the demographics. "Historically, data has shown that only about 20 percent of the population exercises [regularly]," says LaChusa. "Research the population of adults between the ages of 18 and approximately 50 in your area. See if the math makes sense." You can get demographic information from the U.S. Census Bureau (see Appendix for contact information) or contact local government agencies for help.

One of the most basic elements of effective marketing is differentiating your business from the competition. One marketing consultant calls it "eliminating the competition." If you set yourself apart because no one else does exactly

## Bright Idea

Update your business plan every year. Choose an annual date when you sit down with your plan, compare how closely your actual operation and results mirrored your forecasts, and decide if your plans for the coming year need adjusting. You will also need to make your financial forecasts for the coming year based on current and expected market conditions.

**Stat Fact**

More than half the clubs surveyed by the International Health, Racquet, and Sportsclub Association said personal training services were among their five most profitable programs.

what you do, then you essentially have no competition. (In Chapter 6, you'll find more on ways to distinguish your business through serving a niche market.)

However, before you can differentiate yourself, you first need to understand who your competitors are and why your customers might patronize them. With the popularity of the internet, more and more of your competitors will have web sites, which you can visit to find out what type of services they offer. Research what they do, how they operate, and how much they charge.

Of course, offering something no one else is offering could give you an edge in the market—but it could also mean that someone else has tried that and it didn't work. Don't make hasty decisions. Do your homework before finalizing your services.

# The Competitor You Can't See

In most fields, competitors are fairly easy to identify. They are individuals or companies offering the same or a similar product or service to the market you're targeting. Of course, other personal trainers are your competitors. You might even consider some gyms and health clubs competition. But what might arguably be your biggest competitor is an intangible: the quick-fix attitude. People are besieged by advertisements, infomercials, and sales pitches that promise a physical transformation with little or no effort. Take these pills, and your fat will melt away. Spend just five minutes per day using this machine, and in two weeks you'll have washboard abs. Follow this diet, and you'll lose 30 pounds in 30 days.

Of course, these products and programs don't work and may even cause physical harm to the people who use them. And after trying one gimmick after another without success, many people come to believe that they cannot change and are destined to be forever overweight and unfit.

It's a challenging paradox. People know from experience that the quick fixes don't work, but rather than see the fault with that particular approach, they see it with themselves. After all, they reason, it worked for the people in the ads, so if it isn't working for them it must be their fault.

Messages pushing instant gratification for just about everything are virtually everywhere. As a personal trainer, you will be competing every day with the quick-fix gimmicks that don't work and have sabotaged people into believing they can look

▲

## Bright Idea

Don't just take a "me, too" approach to training. Develop your own professional personality, your own techniques, and your own program. Do things that will make you stand out from other personal trainers in a positive way.

and feel great in a short time if they can just find the right product to use. You'll have to use logic and reason to persuade them to take a longer-term and healthier approach.

# The Industry's Showcase

The more you know about the health and fitness industry in general, as well as personal training in particular, the easier it will be to develop an effective business plan.

An excellent source of information about the industry comes from conventions and trade shows. They're tremendous opportunities for education and networking. They're also an opportunity for industry leaders to showcase their products and services.

Two of the leading show coordinators are Club Industry and International Health, Racquet, & Sportsclub Association (IHRSA). Contact information is in the Appendix. Check out their show schedules and invest in attending, even if it means traveling to do so.

# Selling Related Products

Some personal trainers limit their business to training; others take advantage of additional revenue opportunities such as nutritional supplements, exercise equipment, and clothing. Of course, if you have a studio, a refreshment area where you sell bottled water, smoothies, other beverages, and healthy snacks makes sense.

There are pros and cons to each approach. "I don't sell any products," says Jennifer B., the personal trainer in Brooklyn. "When people make a commitment to exercise, I'm very careful about adding on to their commitment or asking them to do something further that may be too much for them." On the other hand, these extra

## Smart Tip

Tip...

Know someone who might be interested in investing in your business? Don't ask them for money right away. Tell them you're working on a business plan, and before you present it to an investor, you'd appreciate it if they could read it and give you some input. At best, they'll like the plan and offer to invest before you ask. At worst, you'll get some valuable input, and they'll let you know they don't want to invest before you have to risk rejection.

income sources can contribute handsomely to your overall profitability and keep you going during periodic slumps. Be careful that any sideline products or services don't detract from your primary business.

# Establishing Policies and Procedures

Many aspects of your business will evolve and change as you get established and find out what works best for you and your clientele. But there are certain policies you should put in place from the very start. This protects both you and your clients from any problems or conflicts due to misunderstandings. These policies don't have to be complicated—in fact, the simpler and clearer, the better.

## Cancellation Policy

Your most valuable commodity is your time, and it's something you can't replace or recover. If a client cancels at the last minute and doesn't pay you, that revenue opportunity is lost forever. A cancellation policy can protect you to some degree, but you must balance it against clients being upset at being forced to pay for something they didn't receive.

Jennifer B. says she started with a very strict policy requiring 24 hours notice for cancellations, but she has become more flexible. "Obviously, things come up," she says. She tries to reschedule when possible, but reserves the right to charge for sessions missed at the last minute. Trainer Lynne W. of New York City takes a similar

---

# Research Insight

**A** person burns calories throughout the day, even while sleeping, due to the energy requirements to keep the body's systems going. This "resting metabolism" expends about 65 to 70 percent of the total daily calories. Depending on activity level, physical activity can burn another 20 to 25 percent. Eating and digesting food—the so-called "thermic effect of food"—accounts for the remaining 10 percent of calorie expenditure. But even this could be variable. In a study published in 2004 in the *International Journal of Obesity and Related Metabolic Disorders*, British researchers found that the thermic effect of food was higher when a group of healthy, lean women adhered to a diet of regular meal frequency compared with an irregular meal pattern.

approach; she tries to reschedule, but if she can't, she charges for sessions cancelled with less than 24 hours notice.

Facility owner Bill S. has as cancellation line that clients are supposed to call if they can't make their session, and the line forwards to his cell phone after hours. "If it's right before a training session, we ask clients to call their trainer, as well as the cancellation line, especially if it's an early morning client."

**Beware!**

Be consistent with your pricing and policies. You don't want two clients talking to each other at a party and finding out that they're paying different amounts for the same service, or that you're applying your policies differently.

## Late Policy

There are two sides to a late policy: when the client is late and when the trainer is late.

If a client is running late, your policy could be that they don't get to make up their time. But if the client has a good reason and is not habitually late, and there is room in the schedule without inconveniencing another client, you could allow some extra minutes at the end of the session. If you have trainers working for you, you'll likely want to take a harder line with their tardiness. If a trainer is more than five minutes late, for example, the session could be complimentary to the client, but the trainer would have to reimburse the business what the client would have paid.

# Dealing with a Difficult Client

**A** chronically late client is a sign you've got a difficult client. Other symptoms include not paying for training on time, constantly complaining that they're not getting results (even though they're not following your professional advice), and not being motivated to push themselves hard enough, says New York trainer Mike Hood. To help deal with such a client, it's important to keep things on a professional level, he says. "By always keeping the professional tone, rather than the 'friend tone,' this allows you to maintain control of the situation," he explains. "And establish at the onset that you take what you do seriously, that you are a professional and you care. Lay down the ground rules for cancellations and set the standard from day one on things like lateness, payment, and what they are responsible for in your relationship in order to achieve the results they're looking for."

Jennifer B. says when she or one of her trainers is late, they make up the time either in that session or in another. Lynne W. says if the client is late, the session still ends on time. If she is late, she tries to get the time in at that session or a later one, or she'll adjust the fee.

"Clients respect a trainer who stays on schedule," says trainer Richard C. "The trainer keeps clients longer, and that's reflected in the income."

Be sure to communicate your cancellation and late policies clearly during your initial consultation so that clients aren't surprised or upset when you enforce them. Insist that your clients respect your time, and make it mutual. Richard likens it to doctor's appointments: "Doctors are so busy that we make sure we make it to our appointments because it may be a couple of months before we can get another one," he says. "That same kind of feeling should exist with the trainer."

# Think About the Unthinkable

The idea that one of your clients may become ill or injured during a session is not a pleasant one, but it's one you need to think about. You and all the trainers on your staff should be CPR and first aid certified.

CPR courses train people to recognize and care for breathing and cardiac emergencies. To maintain your CPR certification, you must take a refresher course annually. First aid certification courses will teach you how to deal with bone, joint, and muscle injuries, heat-related injuries, bleeding and how to move victims.

Beyond being able to provide immediate first aid, you need a total emergency response plan. This plan will serve as your guide for any situation where a person is injured or lives are in danger, from a minor sprain to a major fire. Dialing 911 is not a one-size-fits-all answer.

Your emergency response plan should be basic—sufficient enough to provide the structure that will reduce further injury and save lives, simple enough that it can be remembered and properly carried out. See the sample emergency procedure policy on page 20. You should think through all the possible emergency situations you might conceivably encounter. The idea is to prepare for the unexpected—keeping in mind that there is no way you can predict what is going to happen.

Consider these possible scenarios:

- A client drops a weight on his foot, possibly breaking a bone.
- A client complains of chest pain and shortness of breath while exercising.
- While working with a client in a gym, an electrical short causes a fire in the cardiovascular equipment area.

▲

- While working with a client in your studio, a disgruntled former boyfriend comes in and begins threatening you both.
- While working with a client in her home, her preteen son is playing in another room and manages to sustain a serious cut or injury.

Some of these scenarios may sound far-fetched, but they are common occurrences that could easily happen while you are present. It's important that you think about what you'll do in those circumstances. Have an emergency procedure policy written down so your employees know exactly what to do. This not only educates them, it also protects you from a liability perspective.

Whenever something happens, begin with an assessment of the situation. How serious is the injury? Is the injured person able to aid himself? Is there immediate danger to others at the location (for example, in the case of a fire)?

---

# Sample Emergency Procedure Policy

## WE MOVE YOU
### *Personal Trainers*

Our goal is to provide a safe, comfortable environment for our clients and to design programs that can be implemented without injury. However, we recognize that there may be times when an emergency situation occurs and outside assistance is required. In those cases, we will administer appropriate immediate first aid and/or CPR. If the victim is unconscious, we will check his/her breathing and pulse; then we will follow these procedures:

1. Dial 911. (If two or more staff members are present, one should be sent to call for emergency assistance and the other(s) should stay with the victim to provide what care is possible.)

2. Be prepared to provide the emergency dispatcher with the exact location, the telephone number from which the call is being made, the name of the caller, a description of what happened, the number of people involved, the condition of the victim(s) (i.e., alert, unconscious, etc.), and a description of what assistance or first aid has been rendered.

3. Follow whatever instructions the dispatcher gives you. In many situations, the dispatcher will be able to tell you how to best care for the victim.

4. Do not hang up until the dispatcher tells you to.

5. Once the dispatcher tells you to hang up, return to the victim.

---

Once you've assessed the situation, take the appropriate steps. That might mean administering first aid or CPR. It could mean calling the police, fire department, or emergency medical personnel. If you have a commercial location, be sure your telephone number, address, and directions to your location from the nearest emergency service facility are posted by each telephone. Don't expect anyone to remember these details in a crisis.

When the situation is under control, complete an incident report for your files (see page 24 for a report you can copy and use in your business). Be sure to get the names and contact information of everyone who witnessed the incident; this will be critical if litigation should arise. Describe the incident completely, including details such as exactly what the client was doing at the time (exercising, resting, in the locker room, entering or exiting the facility, etc.) and what the trainer was doing at the time. Include a description of the procedures you took and the results. For example, if you administered first aid and the client declined further assistance, note that. If you administered CPR, called for emergency medical services, and the client was taken to the hospital by ambulance, record that for your files.

# Are You Liable?

In our intensely litigious society, no business owner can afford to ignore liability issues. In Chapter 9, we'll discuss release forms and liability waivers, but it's important to know that these documents alone will not prevent you from becoming the defendant in a lawsuit.

What is the extent of your liability if a client is injured while under your supervision? Your defense will depend on a number of issues, including whether you are adequately trained and certified for the activity involved; the adequacy of your pre-program screening and testing; whether or not the client signed an informed consent, release and assumption of the risk consent form; and whether or not your instructions and advice were within acceptable ranges based on the client's physical condition and circumstances.

Another area of risk is that of nutrition and supplement counseling. "It's important to not go out of your scope of practice," says Tony Ordas, former director of certification for the American Council on Exercise (ACE). "One challenge we've had is educating people that [if] they aren't registered dietitians, they shouldn't be recommending, supplying, and prescribing nutritional supplements."

Many personal trainers are very knowledgeable on these issues through their own personal interest and study, and it's common for clients to turn to their trainers for guidance on diet and supplements. One of the key concerns in these situations is the unauthorized practice of medicine or other licensed healthcare disciplines. Unless you are well-trained and certified, this can be dangerous territory. A lawsuit on record explains why: When a 37-year-old woman died after following her trainer's advice on consuming nutritional and weight-loss products, her family sued the trainer, the club where the trainer worked, the store where the supplements were purchased, and the manufacturers of the supplements. The suit alleged that one of the five substances the trainer recommended contained ephedrine. The woman was also taking hypertension medication prescribed by her physician, and these substances should not be taken at the same time. The suit claimed that the woman told her trainer about the medication she was taking. She suffered a stroke while exercising and died a few hours later. The trainer learned a very painful and tragic lesson.

**Beware!**
Ignore a small problem and it can quickly turn into a major one. If any sort of incident occurs where you have potential liability or if anyone (client or not) threatens to sue you for any reason, notify your insurance company immediately and let them help you through the process.

# Are You on a Mission?

When you're serious about a business, you work hard to develop a mission—that is, you figure out what you're doing, how and where it's being done, and who your customers are. Problems can arise, however, when that mission is not clearly articulated into a statement, written down, and communicated to others. We've provided a worksheet on page 25 to help you get started.

"A mission statement defines what an organization is, why it exists, its reason for being," says Gerald Graham, R.P. Clinton Distinguished Professor of Management and immediate past dean of the W. Frank Barton School of Business at Wichita State University. "Writing it down and communicating it to others creates a sense of commonality and a more coherent approach to what you're trying to do."

Even in a very small company, a written mission statement helps everyone involved see the big picture and keeps them focused on the true goals of the business. According to Graham, at a minimum your mission statement should define who your primary customers are, the products and services you produce, and the geographical location in which you operate.

Jennifer B. says her mission statement is: "To guide others toward the amazing experience of living in their bodies with confidence and joy." Another trainer we interviewed had a mission statement that reads: "We are caregivers. We try not only to physically inspire others, but also to give people the faith to ask more of themselves. It is our mission to promote healthy lifestyle changes in a positive manner until all of our clients' dreams come true."

A mission statement should be short—usually just one to three sentences. A good idea is to cap it at 100 words. Anything longer than that isn't a mission statement and will probably be confusing.

Once you have articulated your message, communicate it as often as possible to everyone in the company, along with clients and suppliers. "Post it on the wall, hold meetings to talk about it, and include a reminder of the statement in employee correspondence," says Graham.

Graham explains that it is more important to adequately communicate the mission statement to employees than to customers. "Sometimes an organization will try to use a mission statement primarily for promotion and, as an aside, use it to help employees identify what business they're in," he says. "That doesn't work very well. The most effective mission statements are developed strictly for internal communication and discussion, and then if something promotional comes out of it, fine." In other words, your mission statement doesn't have to be clever or catchy—just accurate.

Though your mission statement may never win an advertising or creativity award, it can still be a very effective customer relations tool. One idea is to print your mission statement on a page, have every employee sign it, and provide every prospective and new customer with a copy. You can even include it on your brochures and invoices.

Finally, make sure your suppliers know what your mission statement is. It will help them serve you better if they understand what you're all about.

# Injury or Emergency Incident Report

Date: _____ Time of incident: _____ A.M./P.M.

Name of injured person: _____

Address: _____

Phone: _____

Manager/trainer on duty: _____

Location of incident: _____

*Note if it occurred in the client's home or office, at a gym, or your own studio, whichever is applicable.*

Equipment involved: _____

Description of incident: _____

_____

_____

_____

**Emergency procedures taken by staff:**

○ First aid     ○ CPR     ○ Emergency services [police/fire/medical]

Description of emergency procedures and results: _____

_____

_____

_____

**Witnesses:**

Name: _____

Phone: _____

Name: _____

Phone: _____

Name: _____

Phone: _____

Name: _____

Phone: _____

# Mission Statement Worksheet

*To develop an effective mission statement, answer these questions:*

1.  What products and/or services do we produce? _____

    _____

    _____

2.  What geographical location do we operate in? _____

    _____

    _____

3.  Why does our company exist? Whom do we serve? What is our purpose?

    _____

    _____

4.  What are our strengths, weaknesses, opportunities, and threats? _____

    _____

    _____

5.  Considering the above, along with our expertise and resources, what
    business should we be in? _____

    _____

    _____

6.  What is important to us? What do we stand for? _____

    _____

    _____

# Structuring
# Your Business

**B**uilding a business is much like building a
house: You need a foundation, frame, and roof, and then you can
put up the walls and worry about details like furnishings. Let's
take a look at what you need for the foundation, frame, and roof
of your company.

# Legal Structure

One of the first decisions you'll need to make about your new business is the legal structure of your company. This is an important decision. It can affect your financial liability; the amount of taxes you pay; the degree of ultimate control you have over the company; as well as your ability to raise money, attract investors, and ultimately sell your business. However, legal structure shouldn't be confused with operating structure. Attorney Robert S. Bernstein, of Bernstein Law Firm in Pittsburgh, explains the difference: "The legal structure is the ownership structure—who actually owns the company. The operating structure defines who makes management decisions and runs the company."

A sole proprietorship is owned by the proprietor, a partnership is owned by the partners, and a corporation is owned by the shareholders. Another business structure is the limited liability company (LLC), which combines the tax advantages of a sole proprietorship with the liability protection of a corporation. The rules on LLCs vary by state; check with your state's department of corporations for the latest requirements.

Sole proprietorships and partnerships generally can be operated however the owners choose. In a corporation, the shareholders typically elect directors, who in turn elect officers, who then employ other people to run and work in the company. But it's entirely possible for a corporation to have only one shareholder and to essentially function as a sole proprietorship. In any case, how you plan to operate the company should not be a major factor in your choice of legal structures.

So what goes into choosing a legal structure? The first point, says Bernstein, is who is actually making the decision on the legal structure. If you're starting the company by yourself, you don't need to take anyone else's preferences into consideration. "But if there are multiple people involved, you need to consider how you're going to relate to each other in the business," he says. "You also need to consider the issue of asset protection and limiting your liability in the event things don't go well."

Something else to think about is your target customer and what their perception will be of your structure. While it's not necessarily true, Bernstein says, "there is a tendency to believe that the legal form of a business has some relationship to the sophistication of the owners, with the sole proprietor as the least sophisticated and the corporation as the most sophisticated." It might enhance your image if you incorporate, especially if your goal is to contract to health clubs or work with health-care providers or big companies.

Your image notwithstanding, the biggest advantage of forming a corporation is in the area of asset protection, which, says Bernstein, is the process of making sure that the assets that you don't want to put into the business don't stand liable for the business's

## Research Insight

**B**eing an optimist may be good for your health. A 2004 study looked at a group of men and women aged 65 to 85 living in the Netherlands, and found an association between positive outlook and reduced chance of death from heart disease and other causes. The results are published in the journal *Archives of General Psychiatry*.

debt. However, to take advantage of the protection a corporation offers, you must respect the corporation's identity. That means maintaining the corporation as a separate entity, keeping your corporate and personal funds separate (even if you are the sole shareholder), and following your state's rules regarding holding annual meetings and other record-keeping requirements.

Is any one of these structures better than another? No. We found personal trainers operating as sole proprietors, partners, and corporations, and they made their choices based on what was best for their particular situation, which is what you should do.

Jennifer B., the personal trainer in Brooklyn, says she formed an LLC after operating for many years as a sole proprietor because she felt it was less risky and more professional.

Do you need an attorney to set up a corporation or a partnership? Bernstein says there are plenty of good do-it-yourself books and kits on the market, and most of the state agencies that oversee corporations have guidelines you can use. Even so, it's always a good idea to have a lawyer at least look over your documents before you file them, just to make sure they are complete and will allow you to truly function as you want to.

Finally, remember that your choice of legal structure is not an irrevocable decision, although if you're going to make a switch, it's easier to go from the simpler forms to the more sophisticated ones than the other way around. Bernstein says the typical pattern is to start as a sole proprietor, and then move up to a corporation as the business grows. But if you need the

### Smart Tip

*Tip...*

Not all attorneys are created equal, and you may need more than one. For example, the lawyer who can best guide you in contract negotiations may not be the most effective counsel when it comes to employment issues. Ask about areas of expertise and specialization before retaining a lawyer.

asset protection of a corporation from the beginning, start out that way. "If you're going to the trouble to start a business, decide on a structure and put it all together. It's worth the extra effort to make sure it's really going to work," says Bernstein.

# Business Insurance

It takes a lot to start a business—even a small one—so protect your investment with adequate insurance. If you're homebased, don't assume your homeowner's or renters' policy covers your business equipment; chances are, it doesn't. If you're located in a commercial facility, be prepared for your landlord to require proof of certain levels of liability insurance when you sign the lease. And in either case, you'll need coverage for your equipment, supplies, and other valuables.

A smart approach to insurance is to find an agent who works with other fitness-related businesses. The agent should be willing to help you analyze your needs, evaluate the risks you're willing to accept and the risks you need to insure against, and work with you to keep your insurance costs down.

You should also check with industry associations that offer professional liability coverage as part of their membership benefits. For example, Jennifer B. buys her professional liability coverage through an association. Richard C. says associations are probably the best source for professional liability coverage for personal trainers. Rates vary depending on the amount of coverage you want, as well as other factors, but typically you'll pay about $300 per year for professional liability insurance.

Typically, homebased businesses will want to make sure their equipment and supplies are covered against theft and damage by a covered peril (such as fire or flood) and that they have some liability protection if someone (either a customer or an employee) is injured on their property. If you decide to open a studio in a commercial location, your landlord will probably require certain levels of general liability coverage as part of the terms of your lease. Once your business is up and running, consider business interruption insurance to replace lost revenue and to cover related costs if you are ever unable to operate due to covered circumstances. Also, if you use your vehicle for business, be sure it is adequately covered.

Additionally, being a personal trainer is a physically demanding profession, so you should consider purchasing disability insurance in addition to health insurance—especially if

**Tip...**

**Smart Tip**

When you purchase insurance on your equipment and inventory, ask what documentation the insurance company requires before you have to file a claim. That way, you'll be sure to maintain appropriate records, and the claims process will be easier if it is ever necessary.

**Beware!**
Copying songs from different tapes or CDs for use in classes or with clients without paying music-licensing fees is a violation of U.S. Copyright and Trademark laws. So is duplicating a tape or CD purchased from a fitness music company for your colleagues. Just as you wouldn't want anyone to steal from you, don't steal the rights of songwriters and music publishers to earn just compensation for their work.

you're operating a solo business and cannot rely on others to pick up the slack if you get injured or become ill. In general, disability insurance payments will be about 70 percent of your gross income. Short-term disability policies have a maximum benefit period of up to two years, while long-term disability policies feature benefit periods ranging from several years to full life.

It's best to purchase a "non-cancelable contract," which locks in benefits and rates, according to lawyer and business author Steven D. Strauss, writing in *USA* Today in 2006. Avoid a "conditionally renewable" policy that permits the insurer to change benefits or rates. Also, look for a disability policy that defines your occupation specifically, called an "own-occupation disability" policy, Strauss advises.

The insurance industry is responding to the special needs of small businesses by developing affordable products that provide coverage on equipment, liability, and loss of income. In most cases, one of the new insurance products designed for homebased businesses will provide sufficient coverage.

# Licenses and Permits

Most cities and counties require business operators to obtain various licenses and permits to comply with local regulations. While you are still in the planning stages, check with your local planning and zoning department or city/county business license department to find out what licenses and permits you will need and how to obtain them. You may need some or all of the following:

**Beware!**
Find out what type of licenses and permits are required for your business while you're still in the planning stage. You may find out that you can't legally operate the business you're envisioning, so give yourself time to make adjustments to your strategy before you've spent a lot of time and money trying to move in an impossible direction.

- *Occupational license or permit.* This is typically required by the city (or county if you are not within an incorporated city) for just about every business operating within its jurisdiction. License fees are essentially a tax, and the rates vary widely

## Music to Their Ears

**M**any people like to work out to music. It helps them maintain their exercise rhythm and combats boredom. When you're working with clients in their own homes or offices and they want to play tapes or CDs they own, that's fine. But when you use music in a studio, a class, or any other setting that may be deemed a "public performance," you need a license.

Songwriters and music publishers own the rights to their music, and they have the right to grant or deny permission to use their property and to receive compensation for that use. They receive compensation by being members of performing-rights organizations that collect fees from users through licensing public performances of the works. Fees for fitness facilities vary by the size of the facility, the number of students, and the use of the music (background or instructional use).

The three major performing rights organizations in the United States are the American Society of Composers, Authors, and Publishers (ASCAP), Broadcast Music Inc. (BMI), and SESAC. Contact them for complete information on the procedures and costs involved in obtaining music licenses. (See the Appendix for contact information.)

based on the location and type of business. As part of the application process, the licensing bureau will check to make sure there are no zoning restrictions prohibiting you from operating. This is particularly important if you are home-based and clients will be coming to your home for their sessions.

- *Fire department permit.* If your business is open to the public, you may be required to have a permit from the local fire department.
- *Sign permit.* Many cities and suburbs have sign ordinances that restrict the size, location, and sometimes the lighting and type of sign you can use in front of your business. Landlords may also impose their own restrictions. Most residential areas forbid signs altogether. To avoid costly mistakes, check regulations and secure the written approval of your landlord before you invest in a sign.
- *State license.* Many states require persons engaged in certain occupations to hold licenses or occupational permits. Often, these people must pass state examinations before they can conduct business. States commonly require licensing for auto mechanics, plumbers, electricians, building contractors, collection agents, insurance agents, real estate brokers, those involved in repossession, and personal service providers such as doctors, nurses, barbers, cosmetologists, etc. It

is highly unlikely that you will need a state license to operate your personal training business, but it's a good idea to check with your state's occupation licensing entity to be sure.

# Professional Advisors

As a business owner, you may be the boss, but you can't be expected to know everything. You'll occasionally need to turn to professionals for information and assistance. It's a good idea to establish relationships with these professionals before you get into a crisis situation.

To shop for a professional service provider, ask friends and associates for recommendations. You might also check with your local chamber of commerce or trade association for referrals. Find someone who understands your industry and specific business, and appears eager to work with you. Check them out with the Better Business Bureau and the appropriate state-licensing agency before committing yourself.

Many of the business owners we talked with have ongoing relationships with accountants and know of an attorney they can call on if they need one. They also have other advisors. As the owner of a personal training company, the professional service providers you're likely to need include:

- *Attorney.* You need a lawyer who practices in the area of business law and who is honest and appreciates your patronage. In most parts of the United States, there are many lawyers willing to compete for the privilege of serving you. Interview several and choose one you feel comfortable with. Be sure to clarify the fee schedule ahead of time and get your agreement in writing. Keep in mind that good commercial lawyers don't come cheap. If you want good advice, you must be willing to pay for it. Your attorney should review all contracts, leases, letters of intent, informed consent/release forms, waivers, and other legal documents before you sign or begin using them. He or she can also help you collect bad debts and establish personnel policies and procedures. Of course, if you are unsure of the legal ramifications of any situation, call your attorney immediately.

## Smart Tip

*Tip...*

Sit down with your insurance agent once every year and review your insurance needs. As your company grows, they are sure to change. Also, insurance companies are always developing new products to meet the needs of the growing small-business market, and it's possible one of these new policies is appropriate for you.

## Research Insight

**F**or your golfing clients, working with a medicine ball may deliver longer drives. In a 2004 study published in the *Journal of Strength and Conditioning Research,* golfers who combined resistance training with medicine-ball plyometrics increased both the speed of the club head and driving distance (by as much as 19 yards). The medicine ball exercises were done explosively and mimicked the golf swing, and subjects maximized acceleration by releasing the ball at the end of each movement.

- *Accountant.* Among your outside advisors, your accountant is likely to have the greatest impact on the success or failure of your business. If you are forming a corporation, your accountant should counsel you on tax issues during start-up. On an ongoing basis, your accountant can help you organize the statistical data concerning your business, assist in charting future actions based on past performance, and advise you on your overall financial strategy regarding purchasing, capital investment, and other matters related to your business goals. A good accountant will also serve as a tax advisor, making sure you are in compliance with all applicable regulations and that you don't overpay any taxes. You may want your accountant to hold a CPA (Certified Public Accountant) designation. CPAs are licensed, regulated, and insured; their rates will likely be higher than a noncertified accountant, but the enhanced level of service is worth it.

- *Insurance agent.* A good independent insurance agent can assist you with all aspects of your business insurance, from general liability to employee benefits. Look for an agent who works with a wide range of insurers and understands your particular business. This agent should be willing to explain the details of various types of coverage, consult with you to determine the most appropriate coverage, help you understand the degree of risk you are taking, work with you in developing risk-reduction programs, and assist in expediting any claims. Your agent should also understand if you choose to purchase particular types of coverage from someone else. For example, many personal trainers find that the professional liability coverage they need is less expensive when purchased through a professional association or a specialty insurance carrier.

- *Banker.* You need a business bank account and a relationship with a banker. Don't just choose the bank you've always done your personal banking with; it may not be the best bank for your business. Interview several bankers before making a decision on where to place your business. Once your account is opened, maintain a relationship with the banker. Periodically sit down and review your accounts and the services you use to make sure you are getting the package most appropriate for your situation. Ask for advice if you have financial questions or problems. When you need a loan or a bank reference to provide to creditors, the relationship you've established will work in your favor.

- *Consultants*. The consulting industry is booming, and for good reason. Consultants can provide valuable, objective input on all aspects of your business. Consider hiring a business consultant to evaluate your business plan, or a marketing consultant to assist you in that area. When you are ready to hire employees, a human resources consultant may help you avoid some costly mistakes. Consulting fees vary widely, depending on the individual's experience, location, and field of expertise. If you can't afford to hire a consultant, consider contacting the business school at the nearest college or university and hiring an MBA student to help you.
- *Computer expert*. You'll use a computer to manage your business and track client information. Your computer and data are extremely valuable assets; so if you don't know much about computers, find someone to help you select a system and the appropriate software. Make sure they'll be available to help you maintain, troubleshoot, and expand your system as you need it.

# What's In a Name?

Your company name can be an important marketing tool. A well-chosen name can work very hard for you; an ineffective name means you have to work much harder at marketing your firm and letting people know what you have to offer.

Regardless of what type of business you're in, your company name should clearly identify what you do in a way that will appeal to your target market. For example, Richard C. says if you want to a attract bodybuilding clientele, choose a name along the lines of "Muscle Madness Personal Training." If you're going for baby boomers having trouble getting started with a program, choose something less intimidating. In any case, the name should be short, catchy, and memorable. It should also be easy to pronounce and spell—people who can't say your company name may use you, but they'll be less likely to refer you to anyone else.

Many personal trainers simply use their own name and the primary service they provide. One entrepreneur we interviewed simply put her name in front of Yoga and Personal Training, LLC. "That's what it is," she says. "Just to be straightforward made sense to me."

▲

# The Name Game

**U**se a systematic approach when naming your company. Once you've decided on two or three possibilities, take the following steps.

❍ *Check the name for effectiveness and functionality.* Does it quickly and easily convey what you do? Is it easy to say and spell? Is it memorable in a positive way? Ask several of your friends and associates to serve as a focus group to help you evaluate the name's impact.

❍ *Search for potential conflicts in your local market.* Find out if any other local or regional business serving your market area has a name so similar that yours might confuse the public.

❍ *Check for legal availability.* Exactly how you do this depends on the legal structure you choose. Typically, sole proprietorships and partnerships operating under a name other than that of the owner(s) are required by the county, city, or state to register their fictitious name. Even if it's not required, it's a good idea because that means no one else can use that name. Corporations usually operate under their corporate name. In either case, you need to check with the appropriate regulatory agency to be sure the name you choose is available.

❍ *Check for use on the World Wide Web.* The easiest way to find out if a domain name is taken is to try it out and see what happens (a domain name is something like www.inshapetraining.com). You also can check this on hosting sites such as www.register.com or www.godaddy.com. If someone else is already using your name as a domain, consider coming up with something else. Even if you have no intention of developing a web site of your own, the use could be confusing to your customers.

❍ *Check to see if the name conflicts with any name listed on your state's trademark register.* Your state department of commerce can either help you or direct you to the correct agency. You should also check with the trademark register maintained by the U.S. Patent and Trademark Office (PTO).

❍ *Register your business name.* Once the name you've chosen passes these tests, you need to protect it by registering it with the appropriate state agency; again, your state department of commerce can help you. Though most personal training businesses are local operations, many grow to a regional and even national scope. If you expect to be doing business on a national level, you should also register your name with the PTO.

If you want to get creative, brainstorm as many names you can think of, and ask a friend to help. Don't worry about how they sound—just come up with a possible list, and evaluate it later. As you create, think about the mission statement of your business and the message you would like to convey to potential customers so that they're inspired and intrigued enough to check out your services.

An alternative approach is to use some sort of regional or other descriptive designation, plus the primary service category offered. Yet another possibility is that you may decide your business doesn't need a name other than your own.

# Locating and
# Setting Up Your
# Business

Perhaps the easiest and least risky way to start your personal training business is working from home and doing your training with clients at their locations—either home, office, or in the gym they belong to. You also have a number of other options. You can work out a deal with a health club where you contract with them to provide their personal training

## The Franchise Option

If you're considering opening a studio, at least one company we came across offers franchise opportunities. Fitness Together has more than 340 locations throughout the Unites States and five countries. The concept involves one-on-one personal training in a private workout setting. For more information, visit www.fitnesstogether.com.

services. You can set up a mobile unit. Or you can open your own facility, targeted to clients who want personal service but don't want to join a traditional health club, gym, or spa.

If you are new to the industry, a wise approach might be to start small, working with clients at their locations. Build a solid reputation and following first, then look at a commercial studio if you want to go that route.

Be familiar with the various gyms and health clubs in your area. If you find a client who is already a member of a club, they may want you to work with them there. Or you may have clients who want to work with you in a gym setting, and will look to you for advice as to which gym to join.

# Working from the Home

When Lynne W. first started as a personal trainer in New York City, she worked with clients in a gym and paid a fee to the gym for that privilege. Today, she works with clients primarily at their homes.

If you're going to work from home, your space requirements are minimal and your start-up costs can be as low as a few hundred dollars (depending on what office and exercise equipment you already own). You'll need a small area to do your administrative work and a place to store any equipment you might use. A clear space in your living room is all you need if you do training at home, or you may set up a dedicated workout room if you have the space.

# Commercial Facilities

If you're going to invest in a commercial facility, be sure the market can support the business you envision. You need to calculate your investment; depending on the

# Energy Enhancers

**A** long day of training clients can zap your energy. Here are some tips to help you perk up:

○ *Be grateful.* Take the time to think about the good things in your life. Grateful people report higher levels of positive emotions, life satisfaction, vitality, optimism and lower levels of depression and stress, according to research.

○ *Meditate for 5 to 10 minutes a day.* Sit in a quiet place and focus on repeating a word, such as "one" or "trust." If your thoughts wander, don't fret—just gently refocus your attention on your word without judging your performance. Meditation appears to activate the left prefrontal cortex, which is linked with positive emotions.

○ *Try Qigong.* This ancient Chinese practice encompasses postures, breathing and mental focus (one form of Qigong is Tai Chi). A 2003 study published in the *International Journal of Neuroscience* found that participants with high blood pressure who did Qigong for 10 weeks saw a significant drop in blood pressure, as well as in cortisol and other stress hormones.

type of studio and location, you'll need anywhere from $50,000 to $150,000 to furnish and equip your operation. Then figure out how much you can pay in cash and how much you're going to have to borrow. You'll need to do the market research to determine if you can generate sufficient business to service your debt and still operate your company.

The design of your facility is up to you. You might have one large open room with the various types of equipment grouped together. Or you might have several rooms dedicated to specific functions, like a weight room and a cardiovascular equipment room.

Your clients will appreciate clean, spacious locker rooms with showers, toilets, sinks, and dressing areas, as well as a place for them to safely store their personal belongings. If your business is going to be a small studio where

## Beware!

The volume of music during group exercise classes should measure no more than 90 decibels (dB), and the instructor's voice should be about 10 dB louder—no more than 100 dBs total—based on standards established by the Occupational Safety and Health Administration. A class C sound level meter can be purchased for under $100 and will provide a way to monitor sound to avoid damaging the hearing of your clients and instructors.

# Research Insight

**A**re your clients' television habits sabotaging their success? In a Harvard study published in 2003 in the *Journal of the American Medical Association,* researchers reported that every two hours of daily TV watching was associated with a 23 percent boost in obesity and a 14 percent increase in diabetes risk. On the other hand, every one hour per day spent briskly walking corresponded with a 24 percent decrease in obesity and a 34 percent reduction in diabetes.

clients work primarily under individual supervision, which means it will rarely be crowded, your locker rooms do not have to be able to accommodate more than a couple of people at a time.

The facility needs to have a sufficient number of electrical outlets if you are going to be using such machines as electric treadmills. Position equipment in a way that provides a safe, comfortable environment for your clients. For cardiovascular equipment (treadmills, bicycles, elliptical machines, etc.), allow at least 2 to 3 feet of space between each machine. Clients need sufficient space to use the machines without interfering with another client. Have at least 3 feet of space behind each treadmill.

The free-weight area may be the most dangerous place in your facility. If your clients are not using the proper techniques, they could easily hurt themselves or someone else. Be sure they know how to safely handle weight plates, load a barbell, and handle dumbbells. Also, be sure you have adequate floor space for the clientele you'll be serving, and allow plenty of room between benches. The free-weight area should be supervised at all times, even though you may have clients who want to weight train on their own.

Before designing your own facility, visit a substantial number of gyms, health clubs, and small studios to get ideas. Think carefully about the services you're going to provide and what type of environment will be most appropriate.

**Stat Fact**
According to IDEA, an organization for health and fitness professionals, the recommended square footage per person for a group exercise class is 36 square feet; for a step class, it's 40 square feet per person.

# Going Mobile

Another location option is creating a mobile studio. Outfit a van or mobile home with exercise equipment so you can take a gym to your clients' homes or offices.

## Medical Mysteries

Virtually every time you turn on your television or pick up a newspaper, you'll see something about a new medical study that proves or disproves something. You can find studies that say caffeine is good for you and studies that say caffeine is bad for you. You can find studies that claim certain products or activities cause cancer and others that say those same products or activities are totally harmless. If you're confused, your clients are likely even more so.

Most people put a tremendous amount of faith in studies reported by the media. They are also often unable to recognize when someone with a legitimate medical degree is trying to sell them a dubious product, using a medical study as a sales technique. How can you sort out what's real and what's not? Here are some tips for evaluating medical studies:

○ *Find out if the study used animals or humans as subjects.* When studies use lab animals such as mice or rats, the results are not always relevant to human physiology.

○ *How many participants did the study include?* The more participants there were, the greater the chance that the results are valid. A good study will have at least 100 subjects.

○ *Where was the study published?* A peer-reviewed medical or scientific journal is a credible source.

○ *What was the geographic scope of the study and how many researchers were involved?* When tests are conducted only in one place by a small group of researchers, the chances for bias are higher than when multiple locations and more researchers are involved.

○ *Was there a control or placebo group?* Without a second such group, you won't know the true results.

○ *Are the findings ready for immediate application?* News reports of breakthroughs in weight control are common, but frequently the techniques are not available because more testing still needs to be done. Additional tests may disprove the theory.

Decide what type of equipment you'd like to have, then consult with a recreational vehicle dealer or a van conversion or customizing shop to find out how much it will cost you to get the setup you want.

Generally, a mobile studio will cost less than half of a small commercial storefront-type of studio. **Your biggest expense is the vehicle itself,** and that can range from $20,000 to $40,000 or more, depending on how elaborate you want to get. More and more businesses are going to their clients these days, but be sure your particular market will support this service and give you a sufficient return on your investment. A good approach would be to start by visiting your clients in their homes and offices, then, depending on their degree of interest, determine if they would use a mobile studio and be willing to pay proportionate fees.

### Beware!

If you choose to sublet space in a gym or health club, or to contract with another facility to provide trainers, be prepared for the fact that anything can happen to that other business, and the result could range from exciting to devastating.

## Think Personal Safety

Keep your personal safety in mind at all times. If you work with clients in their homes and offices, be cautious when you travel. Let someone else know your schedule, and consider checking in with that person on a regular basis. If you fail to check in, have a plan for what action they should take.

If you have a studio, be sure your reception desk is staffed at all times so people coming in and out are tracked. If you do not have sufficient personnel to do this, consider keeping the doors locked.

# Operating in
# Cyberspace

The internet has changed the way many industries do business, and the fitness industry is no exception. Computer technology is opening up ways for trainers to expand their client base and stay connected with in-person clients. And the internet continues to grow in popularity as more people become used to finding information online. As of

March 2007, there were more than 208 million internet users in the United States, according to the web site www.internetworldstats.com. The U.S. Census Bureau predicted that Americans would average 195 hours of internet use in 2007, up from 104 hours in 2000.

So it's safe to assume that your clients and potential clients will expect you to have some kind of online presence. The computer-face of your business is important because often it will be one of the first impressions your potential clients will have of you. There are several ways you can go online to enhance your marketing efforts, as well as generate supplemental sources of income.

# Setting Up Your Web Site

The simplest option is to create a web site that functions primarily as an online brochure, giving clients information about your company and your trainers. This allows potential clients to learn about you in a relaxed, nonthreatening environment. "They can become interested and already sold on your facility even prior to coming in," explains Bill S., who owns a facility in Atlanta. "If they find something appealing about your web site—if they like the content and the pictures—they'll feel more comfortable. And it provides credibility. When people call on the phone we always ask if they've had a chance to view our web site."

Some web hosting sites offer tools to quickly get your web site up and running—for example, www.register.com, www.godaddy.com, and www.sitesell.com (which has tools to optimize your site so it will be picked up by search engines). You also can use these sites to check if your desired domain name is available. Here are some tips as you think about your site design:

- Determine how many pages you'll have and how you'd like to link them to each other.
- Make navigation easy—for example, users should be able to access major categories on your site from any page within the site.
- Focus on keeping the design relatively simple and easy to read—avoid using big words when a friendly tone will do, and have enough blank space and/or graphics on the page so the reader isn't overwhelmed by text.
- Prominently display your contact information so users don't have to hunt for it—include contact names, your business name, address, phone, fax, and e-mail.

Ideally, a potential client should be able to submit questions through a form on the web site. This also will allow you to obtain their contact information from the form they fill out—just make sure you don't require them to provide so much information that they're deterred from contacting you. For example, require that they give their name and e-mail address, but make providing a phone number and mailing address optional.

# Getting Outside Help

While you can design your own site, you'll save time by hiring outside help, and chances are you'll end up with a professional-looking design. Just make sure the designer builds in some flexibility so that you can make simple changes on your own, especially as your company grows. "As a small business, we wanted the ability to control the content and be able to update the site as necessary," says Bill S., who hired a designer for his company's site. "You don't want to have employees listed who aren't with the business anymore. You don't want to offer or talk about things that are weeks old. That's why the ability to update—at no cost to us—is really beneficial. If we want to change a sentence, we're not dependent upon waiting for [a consultant] to have time, nor do we have to pay a 50 or 100 dollar service fee to do that."

Here are more tips to keep in mind if you hire a web expert:

- When you come across a web site you like, try to find out who the designer is (this is typically indicated at the bottom of the page). You also could simply ask the business directly.
- Keep favorite sites bookmarked so you'll be able to give the designer an idea of your preferences.
- As you're narrowing down your choice of designers, look at their own web sites, and check out their portfolios.
- Consider putting your project out to bid online at www.guru.com, which is an online marketplace touting more than 600,000 freelancers whose expertise includes web design, programming, and graphic design.
- Check to see if your designer can build the site from pre-formed templates—this could save on costs.
- If the developer is building the site from scratch, determine in writing who owns the source code—if the designer does, this could limit what you can do with the site later on.
- Get your agreement with the designer in writing and save your correspondence.

> **Bright Idea**
> To find a web site designer, check with business and networking groups you belong to for references.

## Don't Give Away the Store

**B**e wary of putting exercise tips on your site—if you do so, keep things simple. This will help limit your potential liability and is just good marketing. "You want to give some information to be helpful so that even if they never contact you, perhaps you've motivated them, you've educated them," says Bill S. But from a sales standpoint, he says, giving away too much information for free isn't a good idea because the web surfer should have an incentive to contact you. In fact, that same principle applies to listing your prices. "One reason we don't publish our prices online," he says. "is that we at least want the opportunity to talk to them."

# Computer-Based Training Tools

If you want to move beyond simply having a web site presence, you could consider computer-based tools to enhance your services, either as your primary method of delivering training or in conjunction with face-to-face sessions.

Depending on the features of a particular program, you may be able to assess your clients' fitness levels, plan their programs, analyze their progress, maintain appointment schedules, handle billing and invoicing, and do training online. Online training allows you to give one-on-one attention to clients who may not be able to afford a face-to-face program, and to train clients in different geographic areas. Some services offer web site set up. Here's a sampling of products, but shop around to find the personal trainer software or online service most appropriate for you:

- Pro Fitness PT, www.profitnessgroup.com
- Visual ClubMate, www.aspensoftware.com
- BSDI, www.bsdiweb.com
- Hi-Tech Trainer, www.hitechtrainer.com and www.hitechwebflexor.com
- www.gubb.net
- www.youPump.com
- Crosstrainer, www.crosstrainer.ca
- Wellcoaches, www.wellcoach.com

Another alternative is to design your own online training capability from scratch. Depending on how things are set up, clients could use your web site to complete forms that would allow you to do an assessment and create a program for them. You

# When Trainers Go Electronic

Trainer Mike Hood uses www.gubb.net to create, manage, and share an unlimited number of lists with clients. "It allows you to be mobile while not in a session, while integrating reminders, lists and tips for various parts of everyday life," Mike says. Trainer Louis Coraggio uses www.youPump.com, a membership site that helps you quickly set up an online training business. You get access to a drag and drop tool to create your own iPod workouts and an online store to sell them. "It is an effective way to increase clients and prevent burning out from trying to squeeze a certain amount of clients into a day," he says.

could provide them with an online exercise diary, which you review regularly to evaluate their progress and make adjustments if necessary. Questions could be handled via e-mail.

A good web site designer should be able to set up an online personal training business site for you based on your specifications. Trainer Annette Hudson, for example, had her online training site professionally designed (at www.MyFitnessTrainer.com). But it's not an inexpensive endeavor. "This cost a lot of money, which I funded with my [in person] personal training business," she says. "I won't quit training live until the web site is making enough. If you are starting your own online company, you shouldn't expect it to make a lot of money right away."

## Bright Idea

Computer software also is providing ways for you to stay organized and present a more professional image. Trainer Louis C. uses a personal PDA-based training program from Vesteon Software (www.vesteon-software.com), which focuses on keeping detailed records of workouts, billing, goals, and personal measurements for yourself or your clients. "Forget about clip boards and note taking," he says. "Use a program that is compatible with a pda to document exercise data."

# E-Mail Dos and Don'ts

Sending e-mails to your clients and prospects is an inexpensive way to stay connected. Bill S. sends out weekly or twice-weekly e-mails to his client list as well as people who have contacted the facility inquiring about services over the phone or through the web site. "We send them information on current research findings, recipes, and

▲

## Research Insight

**A** new client may experience delayed onset muscle soreness (DOMS)—the pain from exercise that occurs 12 or more hours after training. This probably results from microscopic tearing of muscle fibers and swelling. Eccentric movements, such as running downhill or lowering weights, seem to the be the worst culprits. Proper warm up and cool down can mitigate DOMS; once the damage is done, it may help to do low-impact cardio because this increases blood flow through the affected area.

other things related to health and fitness," he says. He often hears from people in other parts of the country who were forwarded one of his e-mails, and they request to get on his mailing list.

But be cautious, because e-mail can backfire in this day and age of spam e-mail campaigns. "You've got to be careful because if you're soliciting, people are going to delete the mail and ask to be removed from your e-mail list," Bill says. "Not one e-mail we have sent out in the last three years said, 'Sign up now' or 'We've got this special going on.' Instead, we focus on educating."

# Boosting Traffic

To drive traffic to your site, get creative. Trainer Annette H., for example, ran a weight loss contest on her site. "I was rewarded with a dramatic increase in traffic," she says, "which continued after the contest ended. It was a lot of fun awarding the prizes, which were donated by Bowflex, PCGamerBike, AquaJogger, and others."

Another idea: If you have a membership web site, you can give free trials to new members. "You'll dramatically improve your sign-up rate if you allow the member two weeks to make sure they like the program," says Annette. She also suggests giving web site members inexpensive gifts with your logo, such as pens and calendars.

Here are more traffic-boosting strategies:

- When you use a program such as Google Adwords, an ad for your web site appears next to internet search results based on keywords you choose. You're charged when someone clicks on your ad. "I recommend using the most specific keywords that you can—this will keep the cost way down," Annette says.

## Research Insight

**I**f you have a client who's worried that weight lifting will make her "bulky" and less flexible, you can point to a 2002 study in *The Journal of Strength and Conditioning Research*. Older women who resistance trained enjoyed a 13 percent increase in their flexibility as measured during a sit and reach test—even without performing any supplemental stretching exercises.

For example, if your studio is located in Minneapolis, use the keywords 'Minneapolis personal training' instead of 'personal training.'"

- Use a free online search engine submission tool so the search engines will find your site. The hosting and site-building service at www.sitesell.com has user-friendly tools for search engine optimization.

- Issue a press release about your new site and include the address on all of your stationery, business cards, and brochures.

- Offer to exchange links with other web sites that are complementary to yours—you'll list their link on your site if they list your link on theirs.

# Web Site Disclaimer

As the number of people who use the internet to find information and conduct business increases, so does the volume of related litigation. Disclaimers can help minimize the potential liability from the use of your site.

If you provide links to other online merchants, consider including a disclaimer that you are not endorsing the products or services sold on the linked site, nor are you responsible for the quality or performance of those products or services. If you provide any type of health-care advice or information, your disclaimer should identify the source of the information and state that use of the information is not a substitute for medical treatment. It's a good idea to consult with an attorney to make sure the type, content, and location of your disclaimers are appropriate and effective.

# Setting Yourself
## Apart

The challenges facing clients are many: time constraints, stress, aging, and terrible food options at grocery stores and restaurants, to name a few. It's no wonder that research has shown that only about 20 percent of people who are overweight are successful at long-term weight loss, when defined as dropping at least 10 percent in body weight and keeping it off for at least a year. As a result, millions of people continue to struggle with obesity, despite the media attention on the problems associated with weight gain. At the same time, our sedentary lifestyle has led to muscle and postural imbalances and a loss of functional strength.

Fortunately, the health and fitness industry is evolving to meet these challenges. While that means you have to adapt with the changes to stay competitive and attract clients, it also means that opportunities to grow your business are never in short supply. And with so much happening in the field, you'll always be assured that your work will be exciting and inspiring.

Here we highlight three trends in particular that offer an opportunity for you to enhance your training business. Realize that by thinking creatively and being open to new ideas, you'll begin to see new possibilities for your talents.

# Wellness Coaching

Professional coaching has existed for 20 years, and until recently coaches concentrated on life, corporate, and executive coaching. But now health and wellness coach training programs are appearing, and some personal trainers are beginning to transition their business into coaching. Wellcoaches—an organization that has been a leader in the field and is affiliated with the American College of Sports Medicine—points out that "professional coaches have long been recognized for their skills in helping athletes, sports teams, and executives perform at their best. Now, professional wellness coaches are helping change the lives of people seeking lasting improvement in their health and well-being."

## Playing a Different Role

As a personal trainer, you typically act as the expert, telling your client what to do and how to do it. But a coach plays a different role. Through thoughtful questioning and dialogue, a coach helps to guide the client in finding answers for herself and gain the self-confidence necessary to succeed in adopting a healthy lifestyle.

An important part of coaching is something known as the "stages of change," a concept developed by behavioral experts in helping people to quit smoking. This model reveals that we progress through a series of steps as we incorporate a new behavior into our lives.

These stages of change are: pre-contemplation, contemplation, preparation, action and maintenance (see sidebar on page 55). For any given behavior change, we are in one of these stages. Interestingly, the basics of how people change seem to be similar across cultures in different parts of the world. In fact, Wellcoaches, which certifies health professionals to coach clients in the areas of diet, fitness, stress, and overall health—incorporates the stages of change in working with clients.

# Making the Connection

Coaching can help people overcome one of the main reasons diets often don't work—the person hasn't "yet connected their heart and their head," says Ellen Goldman, a long-time personal trainer who has started a coaching practice. "They logically know that they need to lose weight," she explains, "but they haven't connected

## Ch-Ch-Changes

**H**ere's a rundown of the five stages of change—you'll probably recognize your clients in these descriptions.

1. *Pre-contemplation.* In this stage, the person is not even yet thinking of changing a particular behavior. They're either saying "I won't" or "I can't" do this.
2. *Contemplation.* In the contemplation stage, a person is giving serious consideration to changing a behavior—they may contact you to inquire about your services, for example. But contemplation is not commitment—a person could spend years in this stage without progressing. In fact, two-thirds of the population may be in the contemplation stage when it comes to behavior change.
3. *Preparation.* Now a person is ready to take action within the next month, although he still has yet to make a firm commitment. As a coach, you'll help him discover his underlying motivations and obstacles, and strategies to overcome them. The client will develop a health and fitness vision statement, which is a general assertion about where they would like to be in six or more months, and why. For example, a vision statement could be: "To exercise regularly and get my stress level under control in the next six months so that I'll be able to enjoy good health when I retire in five years."
4. *Action.* As your client begins to implement her plan to achieve her vision, she is in the action stage. Action is not the same as permanent change, and it's typical that a client can experience a relapse.
5. *Maintenance.* In this last stage of change, the new behavior has become habit, but the client must work to sustain the change. He risks boredom, so it's important to keep his health and fitness routine engaging and fresh.

with the deep down emotion of really why it makes a difference to them." The coaching process helps people do this, so that they build confidence and a foundation to work on.

## A Business for Anywhere

Ellen has been a personal trainer for years, but was intrigued by the psychological impact coaching could have on struggling clients. "When I became introduced to coaching and started looking at the psychology of behavior change, I began to see tools that would help people make significant change," she says. "I'm slowly building the coaching practice with the hopes over the next few years of transitioning more hours into coaching and fewer hours into training."

Ellen likes the flexibility of coaching, which can be done over the phone (Wellcoaches has a web-based platform allowing coaches to interact with clients). She's based in New Jersey, but has clients who live in California and New York, and she has worked with clients from Colorado and Illinois. "I love the idea of having a business I can have anywhere," she says.

## The Coaching Session

The length and frequency of coaching sessions varies. Typically, the initial session is about 90 minutes, where the client establishes her underlying motivations and a vision statement. She also will figure out what her greatest obstacles will be, and some strategies for getting around them, as well as three-month and weekly goals. Follow-up sessions can be anywhere from 30 to 60 minutes. Most coaches charge at a rate similar to that of their personal training sessions.

## The Challenges of Coaching

Coaching isn't something you become good at quickly. Becoming a high-quality coach takes months or even years of training and practice. In fact, "[l]earning and growth for coaches never stops, just as for clients—it is a lifelong journey," according to Wellcoaches.

And with the profession being so new, many people don't know what coaching is, so marketing is an important aspect of a successful coaching practice. "Some trainers are jumping on the bandwagon thinking this is an

### Bright Idea

As with personal training, there is a limiting factor with coaching in that your income depends on the number of hours you're willing to work. In order to address this limitation, a coach could work with small groups—working with five or six people who have a like-minded goal, such as weight loss, stress management, or managing diabetes.

easy way to bring in another income source," Ellen says. "They're going to find that it's not so easy, because you're trying to sell a product that people don't understand, and they can't see." At the same time, because the field is young, you can become a pioneer and get in on the ground floor. In fact, there is a parallel between coaching and the early days of personal training when the general public still needed to become familiar with the service. "Now everybody would like to be working with a personal trainer," Ellen says. "I see wellness coaching following a very similar route."

In order to get the word out, Ellen has approached friends who are health-care providers about placing brochures in their businesses. "I'm finding that [in] my community, I'm kind of rewriting who I am, because people know me as a personal trainer," she says. "I have to get out there and say I have a new service that I'm offering."

## What You'll Need to Do

Certification organizations for wellness coaching likely will become more and more prevalent—so carefully check out any particular organization before signing up. Wellcoaches is affiliated with the well-established American College of Sports Medicine, and offers a comprehensive 13-week training program leading to certification.

# Functional Training

Traditional bodybuilding exercises have focused on increasing muscle size by isolating particular parts of the body. They don't typically challenge a person's ability

## Research Insight

It may often seem that your clients are inflexible in their thinking, but don't get discouraged—they are capable of changing. Although it had been thought that the structure of an adult's brain is rigid, neuroscientists are finding that the brain is flexible throughout life. In the book *The Mind and the Brain: Neuroplasticity and the Power of Mental Force*, authors Jeffrey M. Schwartz, MD and Sharon Begley explain how the brain can rewire itself by making new neural connections. "We are seeing," they write, "the brain's potential to correct its own flaws and enhance its own capacities."

▲

to coordinate or balance. The bench press, for example, is done lying down, and generally isolates the chest, arms, and front deltoids, while eliminating the need to balance on the feet while doing the exercise.

But your clients, of course, don't live in the gym—everyday life involves more than isolated movements. Instead, muscles, ligaments, bones, joints, and the nervous system interact to allow a person to perform complex actions. Together these elements make up a "kinetic chain" that makes intricate movement possible.

So whether they're hoisting groceries out of the car or playing a pickup game of basketball, your clients will need good coordination, balance, and flexibility. Therefore, developing bigger muscles is only one aspect of becoming fit. What we're talking about here is *functional* strength, which allows the various parts of the body to work synergistically to make movements fluid, efficient, and less injury prone.

## At the Core

A concept related to functional strength is core strength. In addition to your abdominal muscles, the core consists of the spine, hip, and pelvic muscles. It encompasses deeper-level muscles that help to stabilize the body and provide a foundation for movement.

A weak core can lead to injury, including lower back problems, and reduces the strength of the arms and legs. In fact, in the elderly there is a link between a strong core and balance.

It's no surprise then, that functional, core, and balance training continue to grow in popularity. In fact, the American Council on Exercise (ACE) listed functional fitness

---

# Research Insight

**W**hile clients know that lifting weights will impact their muscles, many are unaware of the effect resistance training has on bones. In a study at the University of Arizona, women aged 28 to 39 performed resistance training for a year and a half. They saw increases of two percent in bone mineral density at the hip and lumbar spine. This is good to know—women represent 80 percent of the 10 million Americans with osteoporosis.

# Function Fix

**S**everal recent studies have shown promising effects from functional training. In a 2004 study at the University of Glasgow, overweight women who went through a 12-week functional exercise program—training twice a week for 40 minutes per session—saw decreases in body mass index and blood pressure. They also reduced the time it took to finish a 20-meter walk, lift a 1- and 2-kilogram bag onto a shelf, and climb stairs. Even more, the women enjoyed improved scores in a measurement of "life satisfaction."

In a 2005 study published in the *Journal of Strength and Conditioning Research*, 119 older adults performed a functional exercise circuit three times a week for 12 weeks. The exercises included the single-leg balance and the superman (laying facedown with arms outstretched overhead, the person lifts their chest and thigh simultaneously). The men and women showed significant improvement in a number of variables, including the sit and reach test, physical functioning, pain, vitality, and number of doctor visits.

In a 2007 study published in the *American Journal of Physical Medicine and Rehabilitation*, 15 subjects aged 62 to 85 participated in six weeks of functional training or strength training using elastic bands. Both groups improved their walking speed, but the functional training group had greater improvement. The functional group also saw greater increases in maximum knee torque while rising from a chair.

and balance training as one of the top trends in fitness for 2007. Related exercise programming and equipment—for example, foam rollers, wobble boards, and Bosu balls—are "among the fastest growing and most popular exercise options," says ACE. So it's likely that your competitors are offering programs and classes with this type of training for a wide variety of clients. You should strongly consider doing the same if a client is an appropriate fit for this type of exercise.

The National Academy of Sports Medicine (NASM), a certification organization, has been a leader in functional training. In fact, their Overhead Squat Assessment gives you an easy and quick way to determine your client's functional strength and flexibility by viewing certain "checkpoints" during the movement. As the client squats with arms overhead, the feet, knees, lower back, shoulders and head should maintain proper alignment. If they become out of line, this indicates muscle tightness or weakness around a particular joint. Through NASM's protocol, you can then program particular corrective exercises to address the imbalances.

# Choosing a Niche

The big chain gyms target a wide range of clients—they spread their marketing net far and wide in an effort to generate business. As a smaller operator, you can set yourself apart from the big guys, as well as other small training businesses, by taking a different approach. You can target a niche market by focusing on a certain clientele—for example, athletes, adolescents, the elderly, or the pre- or post-natal population. Lynne W., for example, is now teaching a post-partum dance class for moms and babies, called Sling Your Baby Dance. By specializing, you'll gain an even greater reputation in your community as someone with trusted fitness expertise.

In fact, marketing expert Debbie LaChusa recommends finding or creating a unique selling proposition (USP) that will differentiate you and your services from other trainers and gyms in your area. "Research feasible specialties," she says. "Feasibility is a two-fold proposition. First, are there enough potential customers to make a business fly? Second, can you create and/or fill a need that no one else is filling? For example, do you live in an area with a lot of stay-at-home moms? Could you cater to that audience at a central location or in their own homes? Perhaps there are a lot of retirees in your area. Could you make a business out of catering to them? Are there any mobile trainers in your area? If not, consider that as an option."

By targeting a very specific market segment, you can tailor your service package and marketing efforts to meet that segment's needs. And as word spreads of your expertise, this will attract new clients.

## Consider Your Strengths and Likes

To consider the niche you would like to focus on, begin by evaluating your own strengths and abilities. Think about what attracted you to personal training as a career. Then draw a picture in your mind of the client you want to train—the person who will be satisfied with what you have to offer and who you will enjoy spending time with. Now do the necessary market research to determine if enough people in the area in which you want to work fit your profile and can afford your services. If the answer to that question is yes, you're ready to go. If it's no, then you need to adjust your services, your target market, or both.

Once you've decided what you want to do and who your clients are, you can put yourself in front of them and start building your business.

If your niche is dealing with special populations such as older adults, you need to become well-versed in the area you're addressing. Many continuing education sources offer the opportunity to do just that. The American Council on Exercise, for example, offers a homebased course called "Specialized Strength Training: Winning Workouts

# Research Insight

**O**lder clients should be encouraged by a study at the USDA Human Nutrition Research Center on Aging at Tufts University. Frail elderly subjects averaging 90 years of age performed eight weeks of high-intensity resistance training. They saw average strength gains of 174 percent, and an increase in midthigh muscle of 9 percent. They also boosted their walking speed by 48 percent.

for Special Populations." The National Academy of Sports Medicine has a series of home-study courses for training seniors, youth, and pre-natal populations. NASM also offers advanced specializations, including the Performance Enhancement Specialist, where the curriculum includes advanced athletic training techniques.

# 7

# Start-Up
Expenses and
Financing

One of the more appealing aspects of starting a personal training business is that it requires relatively low start-up costs—unless you want to open your own studio. So what do you need in the way of cash and available credit to open your doors? It will depend on what equipment you already own, the services you want to offer, and whether you'll be homebased or working out of a commercial location. In general, homebased personal training businesses can cost as little as a few hundred dollars, or as much as a few thousand. However, opening your own studio can run tens of thousands of dollars or more.

As you consider your own situation, don't pull a start-up number out of the air; use your business plan to calculate how much you'll need to start your ideal operation. Then figure out how much you have. If you have all the cash you need, you're very fortunate. If you don't, you need to start playing with the numbers and deciding what you can do without, or you'll need to decide where to look for outside funds. In this chapter, we'll discuss sources of financing for your new business.

We'll also discuss the equipment you'll need to get started. Management and administration will be critical parts of your operation, and you'll need the right tools to handle these important tasks. Your office equipment needs will vary significantly depending on the size of your operation. You'll also need exercise equipment. The cost of such equipment will vary, from very little for a homebased operation to thousands of dollars' worth of sophisticated machines if you are going to open a studio. Use the information in this chapter as a guideline, but make your final decision on what to buy based on your own situation.

# Sources of Start-Up Funds

Jennifer B., the personal trainer in Brooklyn, works at her clients' locations and uses whatever items are at hand as training equipment, so her start-up costs were nominal. She says it cost her less than $500 to register her business and have business cards and fliers printed. Even today, she owns very little in the way of equipment. If clients want or need items such as weights, mats, or aerobic equipment, they purchase those items themselves.

By contrast, another trainer we talked with needed about $100,000 to open his studio; half that went for equipment, the other half for build-out. Thanks to his previous success with contracting to a health club chain, he was able to self-finance his new venture.

Most of the personal training entrepreneurs we talked with used their own savings and equipment they already owned to start their businesses. Because the start-up costs are relatively low for homebased personal training businesses, you'll find traditional financing difficult to obtain. Banks and other lenders typically prefer to lend amounts much larger than you'll need and are likely to be able to qualify for. You might want to start your business on the side, while working a part- or full-time job, so your personal living expenses are covered. But if you plan to plunge into your new business full time from the start, be sure you have enough cash on hand to cover your expenses until the revenue starts coming in. At a minimum, you should have the equivalent of three months' expenses in a savings account to tap if you need it; you'll probably sleep better if you have 6 to 12 months of expenses socked away.

As you're putting together your financial plan, consider these sources of start-up funds:

**Bright Idea**

Looking for start-up cash? Consider a garage sale. You may have plenty of "stuff" you're not using and won't miss what can be sold for the cash you need to get your business off the ground.

- *Your own resources.* Do a thorough inventory of your assets. People generally have more assets than they immediately realize. This could include savings accounts, equity in real estate, retirement accounts, vehicles, recreation equipment, collections, and other investments. You may opt to sell assets for cash or use them as collateral for a loan. Take a look, too, at your personal line of credit; most of the equipment you'll need is available through retail stores and suppliers that accept credit cards.

- *Friends and family.* The logical next step after gathering your own resources is to approach friends and relatives who believe in you and want to help you succeed. Be cautious with these arrangements. No matter how close you are, present yourself professionally and put everything in writing. Be sure the individuals you approach can afford to take the risk of investing in your business.

- *Clients.* If you're a successful personal trainer looking to expand your business, your clients may be potential investors, says Steve Tharrett, president of Dallas-based Club Industry Consulting and a consultant to health clubs. "I know a lot of personal trainers who have clients with a high net worth," he says, "and the clients believe in them so much that they will give the trainers the financing to start up." Again, it's essential that you put everything in writing.

- *Partners.* Though most personal training businesses are owned by just one person, you may want to consider using the "strength in numbers" principle and look around for someone who wants to team up with you in your new venture. You may choose someone who has financial resources and wants to work side by side with you in the business. Or you may find someone who has money to invest but no interest in doing the actual work. Be sure to create a written partnership agreement that clearly defines your respective responsibilities and obligations.

- *Government programs.* Take advantage of the abundance of local, state, and federal programs designed to support small businesses in general, and health- and fitness-related programs in particular. Make your first stop the U.S. Small Business Administration; then investigate various other programs. Women, minorities, and veterans should check out niche-financing possibilities designed

## Research Insight

**F**or busy clients, it's likely that they'll rely on frozen meals at least some of the time. While this isn't ideal, of course—frozen meals can be very high in sodium—the built-in portion control of these foods is a positive aspect. Research reported in 2004 in *Obesity Research* found that women who ate two Uncle Ben's frozen entrees each day dropped more weight and body fat than women who consumed a similar diet but without the frozen meals (Uncle Ben's sponsored the study).

to help these groups get into business. The business section of your local library is a good place to begin your research.

# Equipping Your Business

As tempting as it may be to fill up your office with an abundance of clever gadgets designed to make your working life easier and more fun, you're better off disciplining yourself to buy only the bare necessities. Consider these basic items:

- *Typewriter.* You may think that most typewriters are in museums these days, but they actually remain quite useful to businesses that deal frequently with pre-printed and multipart forms (such as contracts and medical forms). A good electric typewriter can be purchased for $100 to $150.

- *Computer and printer.* A computer is an essential piece of equipment for any business; this is obviously so if you have a web site. It also will help you handle the financial side of your business and produce marketing materials. You don't necessarily need the "latest and greatest" in computing power, but for a reasonable price you can get a desktop computer with the most current version of Windows, a Pentium processor, 1GB RAM, 160GB hard drive, a CD-ROM/DVD-ROM, and 128MB video memory. A high-speed DSL or cable connection to the internet is desirable. Expect to spend about $1,000 to $3,500 for your computer and an additional $200 to $1,000 for a printer.

- *Software.* Think of software as your computer's brains, the instructions that tell your computer how to accomplish the functions you need. There are many programs on the market that will handle your accounting, customer information management, and other administrative requirements.

# Broken-In or Broken?

**S**hould you buy all new equipment, or will used be sufficient? That depends, of course, on which equipment you're thinking about. For office furniture (desks, chairs, filing cabinets, bookshelves, etc.), you can get some great deals buying used items. You might also be able to save a significant amount of money buying certain office equipment (such as your copier, phone system, and fax machine) used rather than new. However, for high-tech items, such as your computer, you'll probably be better off buying new. Don't try to run your company with outdated technology.

Use caution when buying used exercise equipment. You may get some good deals, but you need to be sure the equipment is in good condition and safe. If you don't have the knowledge to evaluate the equipment, find someone who does before you buy used.

To find good used equipment, you'll need to shop around. Certainly check out used office furniture and equipment dealers. Also check the classified section of your local paper under items for sale, as well as notices of bankrupt companies and companies that are going out of business for various reasons and need to liquidate.

Most personal trainers can run their companies with a word processing program (such as Microsoft Word or Corel WordPerfect, which cost in the range of $85 to $400 depending on the version you get); an accounting program (such as Intuit QuickBooks or Peachtree Accounting, which run about $80 to $200); and either a general customer contact management package or a client management package designed for personal trainers, which typically cost $200 to $900. Software can be a significant investment, so do a careful analysis of your needs and then study the market and examine a variety of products before making a final decision.

Most new computers come with basic business software already loaded. If you're running a one-person operation, that may be all you need. But if you want to grow your company, you should take a look at industry-specific software packages designed especially for personal trainers, such as those from Aspen Software or BSDI discussed in Chapter 5.

- *Photocopier.* The photocopier is a fixture of the modern office, and you'll use one to give clients copies of their records. You can get a basic, no-frills personal copier for less than $400 in just about any office supply store. More elaborate models increase proportionately in price. If you anticipate a heavy volume of photocopying, consider leasing.

- *Fax machine.* Fax capability has become another must in modern offices. You can either add a fax card to your computer or buy a stand-alone machine. If you use your computer, it must be on to send or receive faxes, and the transmission may interrupt other work. For most businesses, a stand-alone machine on a dedicated telephone line is a wise investment. Expect to pay $80 to $170 for a plain-paper fax machine or $180 to $800 for a multifunction device (fax/copier/printer/scanner).

- *Credit card processing equipment.* Credit and debit card service providers are widely available, so shop around to understand the service options, fees, and equipment costs. Expect to pay about $200 for a "swipe" machine that reads the magnetic strip on cards. You'll also pay a transaction charge, which might be a flat rate (perhaps 20 to 30 cents) per transaction or a percentage (typically 1.6 to 3.5 percent) of the sale. Expect to pay higher transaction fees for internet sales, because the fraud risk the bank is accepting is higher than with face-to-face transactions.

- *Postage scale.* Unless all your mail is identical, a postage scale is a valuable investment. An accurate scale takes the guesswork out of postage and will quickly pay for itself. It's a good idea to weigh every piece of mail to eliminate the risk of items being returned for insufficient postage or overpaying when you're unsure of the weight. Light mailers—one to 12 articles per day—will be adequately served by inexpensive mechanical postal scales, which run about $25. If you're

---

## Research Insight

Lifting weights benefits muscle and bones, but does it do anything for cardiovascular fitness? Maybe. A 2002 study published in *Archives of Internal Medicine* looked at the effects of a six-month resistance training program on adults age 60 to 83 and found it improved their body's ability to use oxygen by at least 20 percent. The participants also boosted the time they could treadmill walk before tiring by about 25 percent. At the same time, it's important to remember that lifting very heavy weight (the equivalent of your body weight when bench pressing, for example) can put high stress on the heart. Clients with a family history of aneurysms and those older than 40 should take greater care when lifting heavy weights.

averaging 12 to 24 items per day, consider a digital scale, which is somewhat more expensive (generally around $40) but significantly more accurate than a mechanical unit. If you send more than 24 items per day, or use priority or expedited services frequently, invest in an electronic computing scale (for about $75), which weighs the item and then calculates the rate via the carrier of your choice, making it easy for you to make comparisons.

- *Postage meter.* Postage meters allow you to pay for postage in advance and print the exact amount on the mailing piece. Many postage meters can print in increments of one-tenth of a cent, which can add up to big savings for bulk-mail users. Meters also provide a professional image, are more convenient than stamps, and can save you money in a number of ways. Postage meters are leased, not sold, with rates starting at about $30 per month. They require a license, which is available from your local post office. Only four manufacturers are licensed by the U.S. Postal Service to manufacture and lease postage meters; your local post office can provide you with contact information.

## Equipment Maintenance

*Exercise equipment needs daily and weekly maintenance to function properly and safely. Temperature, humidity, usage, ventilation, and friction can cause wear on equipment. See the manufacturer's guidelines for information on necessary internal and external maintenance. Set up schedules and keep logs to document the maintenance that's been done. Check barbells and dumbbells weekly, and tighten or lubricate as needed.*

### Equipment Maintenance Record

Date: _____

Equipment: _____

Work performed:

O Adjusted        O Patched         O Lubricated

O Cleaned         O Repaired        O Replaced part #_____

Notes: _____

_____

_____

Signature: _____

- *Paper shredder.* A response to both a growing concern for privacy and the need to recycle and conserve space in landfills, shredders are becoming increasingly common in both homes and offices. They allow you to efficiently destroy incoming unsolicited direct mail, as well as sensitive internal documents such as old client records, before they are discarded. Shredded paper can be compacted much more tightly than paper tossed in a wastebasket, which conserves landfill space. Light-duty shredders start at about $30, and heavier-capacity shredders run $150 to $500.

# Telecommunications

The ability to communicate quickly with your customers, employees, and suppliers is essential to any business. Advancing technology gives you a wide range of telecommunications options. Most telephone companies have created departments dedicated to homebased, small businesses. Contact your local service provider and ask to speak with someone who can review your needs and help you put together a service and equipment package that will work for you. Specific elements to keep in mind include:

- *Telephone.* Whether you're homebased or in a commercial location, a two-line speakerphone should be adequate during the start-up period. As you grow and your call volume increases, you'll add more lines. For a homebased personal trainer, your phone can cost as little as $60. If you have a studio, you'll pay $300 to $700 for a system.

  Your telephone can be a tremendous productivity tool, and most of the models on the market today are rich in features you will find useful. Such features include automatic redial, programmable memory for storing frequently called numbers, and speakerphone for hands-free use. You may also want call forwarding, which allows you to forward calls to another number when you're not in your office, and call waiting, which signals you that another call is coming in while you are on the phone. These services are typically available through your telephone company for a monthly fee.

  If you're going to be spending a great deal of time on the phone, perhaps doing marketing or handling customer service, consider a headset for comfort and efficiency. A cordless phone also lets you move around freely while talking. These units vary widely in price and quality, so research them thoroughly before making a purchase.

- *Answering machine/voice mail.* Because your business phone should never go unanswered, you need some sort of reliable answering device to take calls when you can't do so yourself. Whether you buy an answering machine (expect to pay $40 to $150 for one that is suitable for a business) or use the voice-mail service provided through your telephone company (prices range from $6 to $20 per month) will depend on your personal preference, work style, and business needs.

**Smart Tip**

If you travel to your clients' locations, turn your cell phone off when you arrive. Don't let your session be interrupted by a call.

Tip...

- *Cellular phone.* Once considered a luxury, cellular phones have become standard equipment for most business owners. Most have features similar to your office phone—such as Caller ID, call waiting, and voice mail—and equipment and service packages are very reasonably priced. Some cellular companies will actually give you a phone for free if you sign a service contract for a year or more; others sell phones from $30 to $500, depending on the features. Airtime service packages vary widely and are changing rapidly. Your costs will depend on how much you talk. Read your contract carefully and be sure you understand what you're buying.

- *Pager.* A pager lets you know that someone is trying to reach you and lets you decide when to return the call. Many people use pagers in conjunction with cellular phones to conserve the cost of air time and control interruptions. Ask

## Office Supplies

*In addition to office equipment, you'll need an assortment of minor office supplies. Those items include:*

○ Scratch pads
○ Staplers, staples, and staple removers
○ Tape and dispensers
○ Scissors
○ "Sticky" notes in an assortment of sizes
○ Paper clips
○ Plain paper for your copier and printer
○ Paper and other supplies for your fax machine (if you have one)
○ Letter openers
○ Pens, pencils, and holders
○ Correction fluid (to correct typewritten or handwritten documents)
○ Trash cans
○ Desktop document trays

prospective pager suppliers if your system can be set up so you are paged whenever someone leaves a message in your voice-mail box. This service allows you to retrieve your messages immediately and eliminates having to periodically check to see if anyone has called. As with cellular phones, the pager industry is very competitive, so shop around for the best deal. Pagers are usually quite affordable, ranging from $10 to $30 per month.

- *E-mail.* E-mail has become a standard element in any company's communications package. It allows for fast, efficient, and traceable 24-hour communication. Check your messages regularly and reply to them promptly. Basic e-mail services, using a standard modem, range from free to less than $25 per month. However, if you choose to have internet access via DSL or cable, you'll pay closer to $50 per month.

- *Web site design and hosting.* Fees for designing and hosting web sites vary widely. Having your site independently designed can cost anywhere from $500 to $5,000 or more, depending on the features you select. And hosting through an independent service can range from $15 to $500 per month.

## Office Supplies

Because what you sell is a service, you'll require very little in the way of office supplies—but what you need to keep on hand is important. You'll need to be sure to maintain an adequate stock of marketing materials, including brochures, business cards, and other sales collateral materials. Have a good supply of important forms, such as: the informed consent, release and assumption of the risk form, the health assessment questionnaire, and contracts. You'll also need to maintain an ample supply of administrative items, including checks, invoices, receipts, stationery, paper, and miscellaneous office supplies. If you're starting out as a solo operator, you should be able to have these items printed for $200 to $300; if you're starting out with a studio and employees, you'll likely need a larger quantity and the price will increase accordingly. Local stationers and office supply stores will have most or all of the miscellaneous office supplies you need. Many certifying organizations will have sample forms you can purchase or use as a guide to create your own.

You'll also need basic office furniture, including a desk ($200 to $800), chair ($60 to $250), and locking file cabinets ($50 to $400). Used furniture is just as functional as new and will save you a substantial amount of money.

## Exercise Equipment

Lynne W., a personal trainer in New York City, started with a few therabands and gradually accumulated other items, such as stability balls and balance disks. She

# Feeling at Home

If a client asks you to help set up a home gym, keep these ideas in mind:

- ❍ *Determine space requirements.* Elliptical trainers typically use less floor space than treadmills. At the same time, an elliptical may require a higher ceiling. Many treadmills can be folded for storage. Adjustable dumbbells and/or resistance tubing also can save space.

- ❍ *Have a ball.* A stability ball is relatively inexpensive, doesn't take up much room, and allows for functional and core exercises. Plus, it adds an element of fun to workouts.

- ❍ *Buy more floor.* Not only does rubberized flooring offer cushioning, it also protects carpet and hardwood floors from sweat. Perform Better (at www.performbetter.com) has interlocking flooring.

- ❍ *Get inspired.* Hanging motivational posters or quotes on the wall can help a client get inspired and stay focused.

teaches her clients not to depend on special equipment, but rather to work with what they have. "Soup cans make great weights," she says. "Chairs are good, so are pillows. I even had somebody working off a toilet seat one day." She says it's just a matter of learning how to give your clients a great workout by teaching them to use their bodies instead of equipment.

Commercial-grade exercise equipment can be a significant investment. For example, treadmills range from $1,650 to $7,000; elliptical machines range from $2,200 to $5,200. Stationary bicycles can run $1,300 to $2,500. Climbers go for $1,700 to $2,700. A packaged set of weights with a rack will run about $1,000, and weight benches go for $500 to $600 or more. See the "Fitness Equipment Checklist" on page 74 for some typical exercise equipment you may want to invest in.

## Dollar Stretcher

Many exercise and fitness equipment and product manufacturers offer discounts to personal trainers, but few will make that fact widely known. When shopping, ask about professional discounts.

## Fitness Equipment Checklist

*The following checklist outlines the basic equipment you'll want to consider having for your personal training business:*

**For any personal training business:**
- ❏ Scratch pads
- ❏ Pulse monitor with alarm limit and stop watch
- ❏ Blood pressure monitor
- ❏ Skin fold calipers or impedance fat analyzer
- ❏ Sit and reach box
- ❏ Heavy duty scales
- ❏ Height scale
- ❏ Fitness screening chart
- ❏ Stability balls
- ❏ Resistabands

**For a personal training studio:**
- ❏ Stationery bicycles
- ❏ Treadmills
- ❏ Elliptical machines
- ❏ Weight benches
- ❏ Weights
- ❏ Dumbbells
- ❏ Medicine balls
- ❏ Excercise flooring

# Vehicle

If you're going to conduct training outside your own studio, you'll need reliable transportation. For most personal trainers, a small, sturdy economy car will be sufficient. If you transport equipment, it will need to be large enough to accommodate whatever you take along.

You can use your own vehicle if it is suitable, or lease or purchase one that will better meet your needs. Either way, keep good records of your automobile expenses because they are tax deductible. Depending on the type of car and driving you do, it will cost you anywhere from 30 to 50 cents per mile to operate your vehicle (that includes the cost of the vehicle, maintenance, insurance, fuel, etc.).

 **Beware!**

Most of the equipment you need can be purchased at retail stores and charged on credit cards—but too much debt can doom your business before it gets off the ground. Only use your credit cards for items that will contribute to revenue generation. And have a repayment plan in place before you buy.

Keep in mind that your vehicle contributes to your overall image, so keep it neat and clean at all times. Proper mechanical maintenance is also important; it's not very impressive when you have to call a tow truck because your car broke down at a client's home, or when you're late to an appointment for the same reason.

To promote your company, consider investing in a magnetic sign you can attach to your vehicle when you're working. When your car is parked in front of your client's house for an hour or so several times a week, that sign lets the neighbors know how to reach you.

# Adding It All Up

The start-up costs for two hypothetical personal training businesses are listed in "Start-Up Expenses" on pages 76 and 77. The low-end estimate represents a sole proprietor working from a homebased office with no employees. He has 20 to 25 clients at any given time and estimated annual revenue of $75,000. The high-end estimate represents a business whose owner has opened a 2,500-square-foot studio serving 80 to 100 clients. This owner has a staff of three trainers (one full time, two part time) and one part-time administrative assistant, and estimates annual revenue to be $360,000.

In addition to start-up costs, you'll also have ongoing monthly expenses to consider. For a discussion of these operating expenses and how to keep track of your financial records, refer to Chapter 11.

# Start-Up Expenses

| Start-Up Expenses | Homebased | Studio |
|---|---|---|
| Market research (including subscriptions to trade journals and professional association dues) | $ 50 | $ 75 |
| Licenses/permits | 150 | 150 |
| Legal and accounting services | 375 | 375 |
| Start-up advertising | 50 | 1,000 |
| Web site design | 0 | 500 |

| Facility | Homebased | Studio |
|---|---|---|
| Lease (security deposit and first month) | $0 | $2,000 |
| Security system | 0 | 1,500 |
| Build-out (including locker rooms, showers, restrooms, exercise area) | 0 | 45,000 |
| Signage | 0 | 400 |
| Utility deposit and phone installation | 90 | 240 |
| Employee wages and benefits (first month) | 0 | 10,000 |

| Exercise Equipment | Homebased | Studio |
|---|---|---|
| Treadmills ($2,000 each) | $0 | $8,000 |
| Elliptical machines ($2,200 each) | 0 | 6,600 |
| Stationery bicycles ($1,800 each) | 0 | 3,600 |
| Climbers ($2,000 each) | 0 | 4,000 |
| Free weights and racks ($1,000 each set) | 0 | 2,000 |
| Weight benches ($550 each) | 0 | 1,100 |

| Fitness Assessment Equipment | Homebased | Studio |
|---|---|---|
| Pulse monitor | $129 | $600 |
| Blood pressure monitor | 65 | 400 |
| Calipers and fat analyzer devices | 10 | 750 |

## Start-Up Expenses, continued

| Fitness Assessment Equipment | Homebased | Studio |
|---|---|---|
| Peak flow meter | 20 | 135 |
| Sit-and-reach box | 116 | 400 |
| Height/weight scales | 25 | 325 |

| Office Furnishings and Equipment | Homebased | Studio |
|---|---|---|
| Computer | $1,500 | $3,500 |
| Printer | 250 | 500 |
| Software | 165 | 365 |
| Desk(s) | 200 | 800 |
| Chair(s) | 60 | 225 |
| File cabinet(s) | 60 | 175 |
| Multifunction device (fax/copier/printer/scanner) | 200 | 350 |
| Telephone system | 70 | 450 |
| Credit card processing equipment | 0 | 200 |
| Forms and office supplies | 200 | 400 |
| (brochures, business cards, informed consent form, health assessment questionnaire, contracts, checks, invoices, receipts, stationery, paper, etc.) | | |

| | | |
|---|---|---|
| **Subtotal** | $3,785 | $96,115 |
| Miscellaneous (add roughly 10%) | $370 | $9,600 |
| **Total Start-Up Expenses** | **$4,155** | **$105,715** |

# 8

# Staffing
# Maximizing Your Human Resources

Successful personal training businesses can range from the small solo operator who works part time, to a company with hundreds of employees. Jennifer B., the personal trainer in Brooklyn, has six teachers and trainers who work with her as independent contractors. "They work other places and do other things as well," she says. Many other trainers work alone.

Whatever size of company you aspire to have, it's a good idea for you to understand the human resources aspect of owning a business.

The first step in formulating a comprehensive human resources program is to decide exactly what you want each of your employees to do. The job description doesn't have to be as formal as one you might expect for a large corporation, but it needs to clearly outline the person's duties and responsibilities. It should also list any special skills or other required credentials (such as specific certifications or education requirements, or a valid driver's license and clean driving record) for someone who is going to work for your particular type of business.

Next, you need to establish a pay scale. Typically, the personal trainers you hire will get a percentage of what the client pays. Administrative staff should be paid according to the going rate in your area for those particular skills.

You'll also need a job application form. You can get a basic form at most office supply stores, or you can create your own. In any case, have your attorney review the form you'll be using for compliance with the most current employment laws.

Every prospective employee should fill out an application—even if it's someone you know, and even if they have submitted a detailed resume. A resume is not a signed, sworn statement acknowledging that you can fire them if they lie; an application is. The application will also help you verify their resume; compare the two and make sure the information is consistent.

Now you're ready to start looking for candidates.

# Where to Look

Picture the ideal candidate in your mind. Is this person likely to be unemployed and reading the classified ads? It's possible, but you'll probably improve your chances for a successful hire if you are more creative in your search technique than simply writing a "help wanted" ad.

Sources for prospective employees include suppliers, former co-workers, clients, and professional associations. Put the word out among your social contacts as well—you never know who might know the perfect person for your operation. Bill S., who owns a facility near Atlanta, looks to hire trainers who share his strong interest in helping and educating clients. "You want to hire people with the same vision and the same passion," he says.

> **Bright Idea**
> Always be on the lookout for new trainers and other employees, even when you don't have a specific opening. Keep resumes and applications of qualified people on file so you have a ready resource in the event of an unexpected staffing need.

Use caution if you decide to hire your friends and relatives—many personal relationships are not strong enough to survive an employee-employer situation. Small-business owners in all industries tell of nightmarish experiences when a friend or relative refused to accept direction or in other ways abused a personal relationship in the course of business.

The key to success as an employer is making it clear from the start that you are the one in charge. You don't need to act like a dictator, of course. Be diplomatic, but set the ground rules in advance and stick to them.

# Evaluating Applicants

When you actually begin the hiring process, don't be surprised if you're as nervous at the prospect of interviewing potential employees as they are about being interviewed. After all, they may need a job—but the future of your company is at stake.

## It's All Relative

**W**hile hiring your friends and relatives may not always be a great idea, once you have some employees (or independent contractors) on board, you may find that their friends and relatives are a source of good candidates.

Why? Because people who currently work for you will provide better referrals than those who don't. Studies show that friends and relatives of a particular employee group will tend to possess values and performance standards similar to those of the members of that group. If you have an outstanding performer, chances are, he or she will recommend others of the same caliber.

Employees will also train and mentor their friends and relatives better than they will strangers. The relationship has already been established, and the senior employee likely has an innate desire to see the friend or relative succeed. Peer pressure is also at work in this situation. Because the reputation of the employee who made the referral is on the line, that person will probably exert substantial influence to ensure that their friend or relative achieves and exceeds your performance standards.

It's a good idea to have a policy prohibiting relatives and close friends from reporting to one another. Be careful not to allow them to be placed in situations where their integrity could be questioned, such as handling money without a disinterested party supervising them.

# Evaluating Certifications

How do you determine the quality of a certification agency? Legitimate agencies will be happy to provide you with information to help you make a decision about whether or not their programs are suited to your needs. Only a few organizations are accredited by the National Commission for Certifying Agencies, the accreditation body of National Organization for Competency Assurance. Whether considering a certification for yourself or a prospective employee, here are some additional questions to ask:

○ *Is the examination nondiscriminatory?* Be sure there are no biases that would allow for an unfair advantage for any group. Ask for demographic data to support the answer.

○ *Does the agency promote ongoing education?* Certified fitness professionals need continuing education to stay on top of developments in their field. Look for agencies that require a number of Continuing Education Units (CEUs) to maintain their certification.

○ *Does the agency have a formal disciplinary policy?* Such policies are designed to protect the public by requiring the fitness professional to adhere to specific standards and policies.

○ *Who serves on the governing board?* Consider the credentials of these individuals. Ideally, at least one member of the board should be a public member— that is, a representative of the people who are being served by the certified individuals.

○ *What are the eligibility criteria?* There should be a logical and appropriate connection between what the certification requires and what the actual position requires.

It's a good idea to prepare your interview questions in advance. Develop open-ended questions that encourage the candidate to talk. In addition to knowing what they've done, you want to find out how they did it. Ask each candidate for a particular position on the same set of questions, and take notes as they respond so you can make an accurate assessment and comparison later.

You also need to evaluate their skills. You might ask a prospective trainer to demonstrate how they conduct a training session or how they would handle a specific scenario. And be sure to check out their credentials. Ask for proof of certification and contact the certifying agency to verify the documentation a prospective trainer provides. With literally hundreds of fitness-related certification programs offered in the United States, you need to educate yourself on the differences.

"Because more clubs and employers are making certification one of the requisites for employment, some individuals will try to take a short cut and forge their credentials," says Tony Ordas, formerly with the American Council on Exercise (ACE). "It's important that employers and potential clients check with the respective certification organization to confirm that the individual is in fact certified."

For administrative and clerical positions, you can administer typing and other tests that allow you to assess applicants' skills and abilities. You can either make up your own test or purchase tests through commercial testing firms or human resources consultants.

Don't accept what candidates put on their resume or application at face value; interview, test, and check credentials to be sure they have the knowledge and skills necessary to produce results for your clients.

When the interview is over, let the candidate know what to expect. Is it going to take you several weeks to interview other candidates, check references, and make a decision? Will you want the top candidates to return for a second interview? Will you call the candidate, or should they call you? This is not only a good business practice; it's also just simple common courtesy.

Always check former employers and personal references. Though many companies are very restrictive as to what information they'll verify, you may be surprised at what you can find out. Certainly you should at least confirm that the applicant told the truth about dates and positions held. Personal references are likely to give you some additional insight into the general character and personality of the candidate; this will help you decide if they'll fit into your operation.

## Research Insight

Research published in 2004 in the *Journal of the American Medical Association* found that walking may help in the battle against Alzheimer's disease. In one study of more than 16,000 women age 70 to 81, those who walked 90 minutes a week performed better on mental function tests than less active women. A second study, looking at more than 2,000 men aged 71 to 93, found that taking daily walks of more than two miles was associated with almost half the risk of developing dementia compared with walking under a quarter-mile per day.

Keep in mind that under the Immigration Reform and Control Act of 1986, you may only hire persons who may legally work in the United States, which means citizens and nationals of the United States, and aliens authorized to work in the United States. As an employer, you must verify the identity and employment eligibility of everyone you hire. During the interviewing process, let the applicant know that you will be doing this. Once you have made the job offer and the person is brought on board, you must complete the Employment Eligibility Verification Form (I-9) and then retain it for at least three years, or one year after employment ends, whichever period of time is longer.

> **Smart Tip** Tip...
>
> Don't expect to find workers who have all the qualifications, experience, and training you want from the start. Look for a solid foundation of credentials, integrity, and character. Then be willing to train people to do things your way.

Be sure to document every step of the interview and reference-checking process. Even very small companies are finding themselves targets of employment discrimination suits; if it happens to you, good records are your best defense.

## Once They're on Board

The hiring process is only the beginning of the challenge of having employees. The next thing you need to do is train them. Of course, a certified personal trainer should already know how to work with a client, but you need to take the time to teach him or her your own policies and procedures, as well as particular training philosophies you follow. Administrative staffers need to be taught your systems and have their responsibilities thoroughly explained.

Proper training in the business's approach helps instill confidence in the trainers, says facility owner Bill S., who requires each of his new trainers to go through a training period of two weeks to four months, depending on the person's experience level. "If they lack confidence and they're out on the floor, the clients are going to see that and they're going to recognize the difference," he says. And because trainers come from various professional backgrounds that may reflect different exercise philosophies, a formal training period helps ensure everyone is on the same page. "It's okay that each trainer has their own personality, but the entire facility should be speaking the same message and providing the same information," Bill says.

Whether done in a formal classroom setting or on the job, effective training begins with a clear goal and a plan for reaching it. Training falls into one of three major categories: orientation, which includes explaining company policies and procedures; job skills, which focuses on how to do specific tasks; and ongoing development, which enhances the basic job skills and grooms employees for future challenges and opportunities. These tips will help you maximize your training efforts:

- *Find out how people learn best.* Delivering training is not a one-size-fits-all proposition. People absorb and process information differently, and your training method needs to be compatible with their individual preferences. Some people can read a manual, others prefer a verbal explanation, and still others need to see a demonstration.

- *Be a strong role model.* Don't expect more from your employees than you are willing to do. You're a good role model when you do things the way they should be done all the time. Don't take shortcuts you don't want your employees to take, or behave in any way you don't want them to behave. On the other hand, don't assume that simply doing things the right way is enough to teach others how to do things. Being a role model is not a substitute for training; it reinforces training. If you only role model but never train, employees aren't likely to get the message.

- *Look for training opportunities.* Once you get beyond basic orientation and job skills training, you need to constantly be on the lookout for opportunities to

## Research Insight

**H**ow important is sleep? Losing sleep affects the prefrontal cortex, whose job includes helping you make judgments and decisions. This was dramatically illustrated in a 2000 study at Loughborough University in the United Kingdom, where researchers looked at the impact of sleep loss on people playing a business simulation game. One group had gone without sleep for 36 hours, while the other group had slept. As the game progressed, the sleepless players repeated trying solutions that had worked earlier but were no longer useful, and they eventually either went bankrupt or came close to it. The sleep-filled players, on the other hand, did fine.

enhance the skill and performance levels of your employees. You can provide the training yourself or send them to continuing education programs.

- *Make it real.* Whenever possible, use real-life situations to train—but avoid letting clients know they've become a training experience for employees.
- *Anticipate questions.* Don't assume that employees know what to ask. In a new situation, people often don't understand enough to formulate questions. Anticipate their questions and answer them in advance.
- *Ask for feedback.* Finally, encourage employees to let you know how you're doing as a trainer. Just as you evaluate their performance, convince them that it's OK to tell you the truth. Ask them what they thought of the training and your techniques, and use that information to improve your own training skills.

# Paying Your Employees

Whether trainers are employees or independent contractors, they typically get a portion of the fee the clients pay. Jennifer B. says her trainers get 50 to 60 percent, although new trainers get less than that until they're up to speed. Her trainers are independent contractors, and she pays them every two weeks.

Another trainer we interviewed had a different arrangement—with trainers paid based on their revenue—the more they bill for the company, the greater their percentage. For a part-time trainer billing $3,000 a month, for example, there is a 50-50 split. For a trainer working full-time and doing well, their revenue may be $10,000 a month, and they would earn 75 percent of that. "We only take 25 percent," he says, "and the facility is still making more off that trainer than the one who is billing less and we're getting 50 percent from."

When you set a payment structure that lets your superstars make a substantial income, you accomplish two important things: You keep them working hard, because they're being rewarded, and you give them the incentive to stay with you rather than moving elsewhere or opening their own businesses. If the trainer is an employee and has other responsibilities in addition to working with clients, you might want to pay them a small hourly rate plus a percentage of their clients' fees.

## Employee Benefits

The actual wages you pay may be only part of your employees' total compensation. While many very small companies do not offer a formal benefits program, more and more business owners have recognized that benefits—particularly medical insurance—are extremely important when it comes to attracting and retaining quality employees. Offering a benefits package makes you more attractive to prospective employees.

Typical benefits packages include group insurance (your employees may pay all or a portion of their premiums), paid holidays, and vacations. You might offer year-end bonuses based on the company's profitability. You can build employee loyalty by seeking additional benefits that may be somewhat unusual—and they don't have to cost much. For example, if you're in a retail location, talk to other storekeepers in the area to see if they're interested in providing reciprocal employee discounts. You'll not only provide your own employees with a benefit, but you may get some new customers out of the arrangement.

> **Bright Idea**
>
> If you have employees, consider using a payroll service rather than trying to handle this task yourself. The service will calculate taxes; handle reporting and paying local, state, and federal payroll taxes; make deductions for savings, insurance premiums, and loan payments; and may offer other benefits to you and your employees.

One type of insurance may not be optional. In most states, if you have three or more employees, you are required by law to carry workers' compensation insurance. This coverage pays medical expenses and replaces a portion of the employee's wages if he or she is injured on the job. Details and requirements vary by state; contact your state's insurance office or your own insurance agent for information so you can be sure to be in compliance.

Beyond tangible benefits, look for ways to provide positive working conditions. Consider flexible working hours, establish family-friendly policies, and be sure the physical environment is comfortable and designed to enhance productivity.

# Employees or Independent Contractors?

An important part of the hiring process is deciding whether you want to hire employees of your own or go with independent contractors. There are advantages and disadvantages to both approaches. What's important is that you clearly understand the difference so you can avoid unnecessary and costly mistakes when it comes to tax time.

As an employer, you have greater control over employees than you do over independent contractors. Employees must comply with company policies, and with instructions and direction they receive from you or a manager. As a result, you'll be more likely to have all of

> **Beware!**
>
> Before you hire your first employee, make sure you are prepared. Have all your paperwork ready, know what you need to do in the way of tax reporting, and understand all the liabilities and responsibilities that come with having employees.

the trainers in your facility deliver a common message to clients than in the case of using independent contractors. Also, you can set their hours and other conditions of employment, along with their compensation packages. Of course, you must also pay payroll taxes, workers' compensation insurance, unemployment benefits, and any other employee benefits you may decide to offer.

**Smart Tip**

Before allowing independent contractors to use your facility or work with your clients, obtain proof of certification and insurance. Verify the proof by checking with the certifying agency and the insurance company.

The IRS has established guidelines to assist you in determining the appropriate tax status of someone who is working for you. Essentially, you need to examine the relationship between the worker and the business in three primary categories: behavioral control, financial control, and the type of relationship itself.

Behavioral control means that the business has a right to direct and control how the work is done, through instructions, training, or other means. Financial control deals with issues related to the business aspects of the worker's job. This includes the extent to which the worker is reimbursed for business expenses, the extent of the worker's investment in the business, the extent to which the worker makes services available to the relevant market, how the business pays the worker, and the extent to which the worker can realize a profit or incur a loss. Finally, the type of the relationship includes written contracts describing the relationship; the extent to which the worker is available to perform services for other similar businesses; whether the business provides the worker with employee-type benefits, such as insurance, a pension plan, vacation pay, or sick pay; and the permanency of the relationship. For more information, consult your accountant or tax advisor, or see Publication 15-A, *Employer's Supplemental Tax Guide*, which is available from the IRS.

**Beware!**

As unpleasant as it may be, it's important to address employment problems early—such as showing up late or not being properly prepared ahead of time to train clients. Letting these situations go unchecked can make for even more aggravation down the road.

# Noncompete and Confidentiality Agreements

To protect your company from an employee or independent contractor leaving you to start their own company that directly competes with you, you may want to ask everyone who comes to work for you to sign a noncompete agreement. Noncompete agreements typically consist of time, geography, and industry restrictions, and their enforceability varies by state. Have the language of your noncompete checked by an attorney familiar with employment law before you ask anyone to sign it.

Jennifer B. says the noncompete that her trainers sign basically stipulates that the client belongs to the company. "It's more of a good faith thing that says 'I wish you to respect my work,'" she says.

Keep in mind that even though your employees sign noncompete agreements, they may choose to violate them. Then you have to make the decision whether or not to take the issue to court.

# Building Client
# Relationships

**B**efore you actually begin training a client, you need to establish the foundation of your relationship, and that begins with gathering personal data, information on their current state of health, their goals for a training program, and other details you may deem necessary. This information tells you what you need to know to develop an appropriate and

▲

effective program. Equally important, it can protect you against a claim of professional negligence. In this chapter, we'll discuss initial consultations with new clients, the necessary forms you'll need to keep on file, as well as how to maintain your client relationships once they're off the ground.

# The Initial Consultation

The initial consultation will set the foundation for the relationship you will have with your client. It's a time for you both to decide if you want to work with each other. It's also your chance to show a prospective client that the value of your service far outweighs the cost of your fees.

Set up a confidential file for each client. To gather the basic contact information you should include when you set up your file, consider having your clients fill out a form similar to the "Client Information" form on page 101. You may opt to maintain much of your information in a database, and that can increase your efficiency. However, you'll still need some paper files with signatures so your clients can acknowledge that you have discussed certain aspects of their health and the training programs with them. Maintain the paper files in locked, fireproof cabinets and password-protect your electronic files.

Much of your initial consultation will involve asking questions. While you need to gather information, you should take care not to appear as though you are conducting an inquisition. Clients can often complete much of the health history information themselves (see the sample "Health History" form on pages 108–110). Then you can review the form and ask any clarifying questions that may be necessary.

The initial consultation also lets you determine if the prospective clients' goals are realistic and if you can truly help them. "I tell them honestly whether I can help them or not," says Jennifer B., the personal trainer from Brooklyn. "I'm sincere. I don't try to sell them something they're not going to be able to do." You also want to find out how the prospective client feels about exercise and fitness (see the "Exercise History and Attitude" form on pages 104–106).

When discussing a client's goals, phrase your questions in a way that establishes the value of what you're going to do for them. For example, ask things such as "How would losing weight affect your current lifestyle?" or "You said you wanted to fit into a size six again. Why is that important to you?"

Finally, you want to use your initial meeting to determine if your prospective client can safely

## Smart Tip

Keep files on people who go through your initial consultation but don't sign up as clients. Put their names and contact information in a database for follow-up marketing at a later time.

*Tip...*

# Every Shape and Size

**B**e sensitive to your clients' emotions and feelings. Many people who are extremely overweight and out of shape view personal trainers with conflicting thoughts. On the one hand, they want you to be fit because that demonstrates you know what you're doing. On the other hand, they may find you intimidating because they think they can never get their own bodies into the same condition as yours. These same clients might also be very uncomfortable doing their workouts in front of others, such as in a gym or club.

Emotions and feelings should also be factored into your testing protocols. Personal trainer Richard C. recalls, "When I graduated with my master's degree, I hit the ground running with my calipers and thought that everyone needed to have their body fat tested. It took me a while to learn this, but that turns a lot of people off. Today, I can sit down with any client and give them just as good a program without testing them, just by asking the right questions. A lot of people like to be tested, and they can handle it. But for others, it can be incredibly demotivating.

embark on an exercise program. After reviewing their answers to your medical screening form, you may suggest that they see their doctor before beginning any exercise regime (see the "Medical Screening" form on page 107). A sample letter to send to a client's doctor is also included (see the "Medical Release" form on pages 102–103).

One trainer we spoke with recalls when he had to refuse to train a client because of his health. "He was a 50-year-old gentleman who smoked, was overweight, had high blood pressure and diabetes, and a history of heart problems in his family," he says. "I told him I couldn't train him at all until he had a complete physical and his doctor called me personally. He never came back." Most people don't like being told they need to see their doctors, he adds, but they will usually take your advice if you are firm about it.

## As the Boss

Keep in mind that when you have trainers working for you, you still have a responsibility to the clients they are training, even though you are not personally training them. Jennifer B.

## Bright Idea

The FDA has a variety of electronic mailing lists to keep you up-to-date about the agency's activities and the products it regulates. You can use this information to help keep your clients informed about issues that affect them. Subscribe by using the links at www.fda.gov.

## Research Insight

In a 2003 survey commissioned by Hilton Hotels and Resorts, business travelers who made time for exercise on their trip out-performed non-exercisers by 61 percent when tested for reaction and alertness. The survey also found that two-thirds of the participating travelers exercised as a way to boost their alertness, performance, and energy while on the road.

meets with every new client before that client is assigned to a particular trainer or teacher. Then she makes a follow-up call every month to make sure everything is going well and the client is satisfied.

# Critical Documents

Certainly you can keep as much paper information as you want on file, but there are several documents that are absolutely essential. You should have on file an informed consent, release and assumption of the risk form signed by the client, a physician release form, and a fitness assessment, in addition to any other critical client records.

## Informed Consent, Release, and Assumption of the Risk

This form states that the client is agreeing to participate in exercise testing and the training program that is developed as a result, and includes a release and assumption of the risk. You should have a client's written consent before putting them through any procedure. In general, the following elements are required for a valid form (although again, it's a good idea to have an attorney review this and other client forms):

- The person must be over 18 and otherwise legally capable of giving consent. For clients under 18, you need the signature of a parent or guardian.
- A statement that the client fully understands all the risks and benefits associated with the procedure and/or program, and a release.
- A statement that the consent is given freely and voluntarily, and not under duress or a misrepresentation of facts.

Such a form should only be signed after a discussion of all the risks and benefits of a procedure or program. Give the client a chance to ask questions, and be sure you've answered all questions completely and to their satisfaction. If appropriate, make additional notes on the form to document any issues that may be raised at a later time. Give the client a copy of the signed form and keep the original in your files.

Of her consent and release form, Jennifer B. says, "When I ask someone to read it, I say, 'You're in charge of what feels right and doesn't feel right. If something doesn't feel right, we don't have to push through it. We'll figure out something else.' I invite them to be in charge of making choices for themselves. I also tell them that I have lots of ideas, and if one doesn't work, we'll find some other way to achieve the results they want."

> ## Smart Tip
> *Tip...*
>
> Perform a regular client attitude inventory. Your clients should be comfortable with you and pleased with their program. If they're not, figure out what the issue is before you have a serious problem. A once-a-week attitude assessment will alert you to potential difficulties while they are still manageable.

---

# Research Insight

**B**y helping a client become fitter and healthier, you may not just be giving him a better quality of life—you also may be adding some get-up-and-go to his career. Here's what researchers are finding about the link between work and fitness:

A 2005 British study surveyed 200 employees who often made exercise part of their work days. A majority of the workers believed that their time management skills, mental performance, and potential to satisfy deadlines improved on days they worked out.

A two-year study published in 2003 in the *American Journal of Health Promotion* concluded that General Motors employees who were obese had $1,500 more in annual medical costs than workers with a healthy weight.

Another 2003 study by researchers at Ball State University in Muncie, Indiana, surveyed 366 small-business owners and found that entrepreneurs who ran enjoyed better sales than non-runners. Also, those business people who ran or lifted weights showed greater personal satisfaction, independence, and autonomy.

See the "Informed Consent, Release and Assumption of the Risk" form that we've included on page 111. You may also want your clients to sign a general "Client Release" form, such as the one provided on page 103.

**Smart Tip**

Be careful not to talk about yourself too much. Certainly your clients will want to get to know you personally, but too much ego can destroy your relationships. Focus on your clients; ask how they're doing, and listen to their answers.

## Physician Consent/Clearance

You should insist on medical clearance for any client considered high risk, and in some cases, for clients who are considered moderate risk. You can assess risk levels by reviewing their health history, medical screening, and exercise history forms. If you feel a physician's clearance is necessary for a particular client, you should request it—and it should be reviewed and updated periodically. Again, see the "Medical Release" form on pages 102–103.

## Fitness Assessment

No one should begin an exercise program without first being sure they are physically able to participate in the program without injury or harm. It would be foolhardy of a personal trainer to allow any client to begin exercising without first doing a fitness assessment and health screening.

By screening your clients using forms such as those in this chapter, you'll be able to determine if they can safely embark on an exercise program. You'll also be able to determine their current level of fitness as well as their goals, which will help you to develop an appropriate program. The initial assessment should be repeated periodically as a monitoring and progress tool, as well as a way to motivate your clients.

## Client Records

In addition to the critical documents we've discussed, you'll need to maintain a wide range of important information on each client. You can do this with paper records or enter the information into an electronic database. You should maintain detailed documentation on all actions, observations, program prescriptions, and discussions with clients. Be sure to record any special instructions given to clients, any warnings or limitations conveyed, progress notes, details of instruction (and instances in which you had to do repeat instruction) of techniques, equipment use or other concerns, and information on any injuries, including details of first aid that had to be administered as a result of an injury.

# Keeping Your Clients Motivated

Tip...

**Smart Tip**
Maintain contact with your clients outside their regular training sessions. Send birthday cards, cards at various holidays, or "attaboy" cards when they've reached a certain goal. Clip articles that you think may be of interest. Let them know they are important to you as individuals, not just as a source of income.

If you're going to maintain a solid roster of clients, you need to be providing them with something they can't get by exercising on their own—motivation and encouragement. One of the most important services you as a personal trainer can provide is to help your clients stay motivated. In addition to exercise instruction, people who turn to personal trainers also need encouragement. Clients who are motivated will stay with their programs—and with you—longer.

Some of the ways you can help keep your clients on track include:

- *Listening*. Listen actively and effectively to what your clients are saying—and not saying. Be alert for verbal clues that will help you identify unspoken agendas.

- *Understanding their motivation style*. After a few sessions with a client, you should have a sense of whether that person is extrinsic (that is, they need you to assist with developing strategies that will keep them motivated) or intrinsic (self-motivated).

- *Demonstrating empathy and compassion, and providing positive reinforcement*. Many of your clients won't have much in the way of a support network and may feel

## Research Insight

How much does advancing age affect athletic performance? When it comes to endurance, maybe not as much as you might think. In a 2007 study published in the *International Journal of Sport Medicine*, German researchers looked at age-related changes in endurance performance of marathon and half-marathon finishers. There were not significant age-related losses in endurance performance before age 50. What's more, age-related performance decreases of those 50 to 69 years old were only in the range of 2.6 to 4.4 percent per decade. According to the researchers, the results suggest that most older athletes can "maintain a high degree of physical plasticity."

like they are fighting their health and fitness battle alone. Let them know you understand and are pulling for them. When they make a behavioral change—even though it may not be as significant as it ultimately needs to be—be supportive.

- *Using humor.* A significant number of your clients exercise not because they enjoy it, but because they know they need to do it for various reasons. Adding appropriate, tasteful humor to a workout helps the time pass more quickly and makes the session more enjoyable.

- *Being flexible and creative.* Clients will become bored with the same routine, so change their programs regularly to keep them interested.

- *Educating yourself and your clients.* While you may have extensive professional training, chances are most of your clients know little more about fitness than what they read, see, and hear through the popular media. Pay attention to news reports, do some additional research to get the real facts, and discuss these issues with your clients during your sessions. And realize that teaching your clients why proper exercise technique is important will help them achieve long-term success. "I would never want to have a client for several years knowing that I was able to help them accomplish their goals," says New York trainer Mike H., "and then have them go out on their own . . . and fail. They need to be able to ultimately take what you taught them and apply it to everyday life."

- *Measuring and tracking progress.* Create progress charts so your clients can see at a glance how they're doing. It's also a good idea to do periodic assessments, which can help you decide on what changes might be needed and also allows clients to see their progress. The best motivator in the world is a program that works.

- *Helping remove barriers.* Your clients are coping with a wide range of mental and physical barriers to exercise. Help them identify these barriers, then come up with strategies to remove them. By becoming trained in the principles of wellness coaching, as described in Chapter 6, you'll improve your ability to do this.

# Can Clients Reach You?

Voice mail is one of the most popular modern business conveniences and can be a significant communication tool. Even so, whenever possible, answer your phone yourself—and insist that your staffers do likewise. Handle calls as quickly and efficiently as possible. When clients call with a question or concern about their health or fitness program, they want to speak to a person, not a recording device.

**Bright Idea**
Periodically call your voice mail to see how it sounds. Make sure what your clients hear is clear and professional.

# Etiquette Essentials

**F**rom a client's perspective, you're demeanor says a lot about how dedicated you are to their success. So it's essential that you practice proper etiquette to make your clients feel appreciated—and eager to work with you.

○ *With a new client, ask their permission before making physical contact, and always avoid certain body areas, such as the pelvis.* As you gain experience with the person, you won't always need to ask because the appropriate barrier will become clear.

○ *Stay friendly but professional.* Dating clients should be out, as should be socializing except in a business context. A client who is the trainer's friend may tend to no longer work as hard because they think their trainer/friend won't hold them accountable.

○ *Don't socialize with others while training,* and don't listen to your iPod (yes, we've heard a story of a trainer listening to tunes while with a client). And don't eat or drink during a session, other than water. If yours clients do see you eat, make it healthy—remember, you're a role model.

○ *Only take cell phone calls if it's an emergency.* If you do take a call, first ask your client if it's okay.

○ *Don't sit.* Not only is it more difficult to check your client's form while you're in a seated position, it sends a message to your client that you're not excited to be training them.

○ *If you use humor as a relationship-building strategy,* avoid political, racial, or sexist jokes or comments. Inappropriate or offensive humor can quickly destroy a relationship you have taken a long time to build.

Some other things to keep in mind:

• *If you use an automated answering system, be sure to tell callers how to reach a live person.* Ideally, that information should come very early in your announcement. For example, your greeting might sound something like this:

"Thank you for calling Personal Training Specialists. If you know the extension of the person you are calling, you may enter it now. To reach an operator, dial 0 at any time during this message. If you are a current client and need to speak to someone, press 1. To schedule a tour of our facility, press 2. For information on our hours and location, press 3. For accounting, press 4. For a staff directory, press 5."

▲

- *Whether you're a one-person show or you have a sizable staff, change your individual voice-mail announcements daily.* Callers need to know whether you're in the office or out, and whether they're likely to hear back from you in five minutes or five hours. Avoid saying the obvious, "I'm either away from my desk or out of the office"—well, of course! If you were at your desk, you'd be answering your phone. And always let callers know how to reach a live person when you're not available. Here's a sample individual voice-mail announcement for when you're in the office:

  > "You have reached the voice-mail box for Jane Smith, and it's Monday, June 1. I'm in the studio today but unavailable at the moment. Leave your name, number, and the reason for your call, and I'll get back to you within an hour. If you need to speak with someone immediately, press 0 and ask the operator to connect you with Bob White."

  If you're going to be out most of the day working with clients, try something like this:

  > "This is the voice-mail box for Mike Green. It's Wednesday, January 23. I'm scheduled to be out of the office from 9 A.M. until 3:30 P.M. with clients, then I'll be in until 6 P.M. I'll be checking messages throughout the day, so leave your name, number, and the reason for your call, and I'll get back to you as soon as possible. If you need to speak with someone immediately, press 0 and ask the operator to connect you with Susan Gibson."

  Of course, if you're a solo operator, you can't include an alternate contact, so just ask callers to leave a message.

# Client Information

Name: _____ Date: _____

Address: _____

Phone (day): _____ (evening): _____

Age: _____ Birth date: _____ Gender: ❑ Male ❑ Female

Occupation: _____

Employer: _____


Emergency contact: _____ Relationship: _____

Address: _____

Phone (day): _____ (evening): _____


Primary care physician: _____

Phone: _____


How did you hear about us?: _____

_____

# Medical Release

Date: _____

[insert physician name and address]

_____

_____


Dear Doctor:

Your patient, _____, wishes to begin a personalized training program. The activities will include:

Exercise type: _____

Exercise frequency: _____

Exercise duration: _____

Exercise intensity: _____


If your patient is taking any medications that will affect his/her heart rate response to exercise, please indicate the details:

Type of medication: _____
Impact on heart rate response to exercise: _____

Type of medication: _____
Impact on heart rate response to exercise: _____

Type of medication: _____
Impact on heart rate response to exercise: _____


Please describe any recommendations or restrictions that are appropriate for your patient in this exercise program: _____

_____

_____

_____

_____

_____

## Medical Release, continued

Please complete the information below and return this letter to me using the enclosed reply envelope. If you have any questions, feel free to call me at your convenience.

Sincerely,
[your name]
[company name]
[phone number]

Physician completes:

_____ has my approval to begin an exercise program with the recommendations or restrictions indicated above.

Signature: _____

Date: _____  Phone: _____

## Client Release

I know of no physical or medical condition that either myself, or my physician, is aware of that could be aggravated by participating in an exercise program. I agree to advise [name of your company] in writing if this changes or if my physician advises me to stop, reduce, or otherwise adjust my exercise routine.

I will advise [name of your company] if I injure myself in any way while on their property or while participating in exercises under the supervision of one of their trainers.

Signature: _____

Print name: _____

Date: _____

# Exercise History and Attitude

Name: _____ Date: _____

Address: _____

Phone (day): _____ (evening): _____

Age: _____ Birth date: _____ Gender: ❏ Male ❏ Female

Rate your exercise level on a scale of 1 to 10 (1 indicating sedentary, 10 indicating very strenuous) for each age range through your present age:

15–20 _____

21–30 _____

31–40 _____

41–50+ _____

Were you an athlete in high school or college? ❏ Yes ❏ No

If yes, please describe the sport and level of participation: _____

_____

_____

Do you have any negative feelings toward physical activity programs?

❏ Yes ❏ No

If yes, please explain: _____

_____

Have you had a bad experience with a physical activity program? ❏ Yes ❏ No

If yes, please explain: _____

_____

Do you have any negative feelings toward fitness testing and evaluation?

❏ Yes ❏ No

If yes, please explain: _____

_____

Have you had a bad experience with fitness testing and evaluation?

❏ Yes ❏ No

If yes, please explain: _____

_____

# Exercise History and Attitude, continued

On a scale of 1 to 10 (1 being the lowest, and 10 being the highest), rate yourself in the following areas:

Your present athletic ability: _____

Your present cardiovascular capacity: _____

Your present muscular capacity: _____

Your present flexibility capacity: _____

When you exercise, how important is competition?: _____

Do you start exercise and fitness programs and then find yourself unable to stick with them? ☐ Yes ☐ No

How much time are you willing/able to devote to an exercise program?
Minutes per day _____
Days per week _____

Are you currently involved in an exercise program? ☐ Yes ☐ No
If yes, please describe: _____

_____

_____

How long have you been exercising regularly?: _____

What exercise, sport, or recreational activities have you participated in?

_____

In the past 6 months: _____

_____

In the past 5 years: _____

_____

Are you able to exercise during your workday? ☐ Yes ☐ No
If yes, please describe when and what type of exercise you can do: _____

_____

_____

_____

## Exercise History and Attitude, continued

Would an exercise program benefit you professionally?  ❒ Yes  ❒ No

Rate your interest in the following types of exercise on a scale from 1 to 10
(1 being no interest, 10 being very high interest):

| | |
|---|---|
| Walking | _____ |
| Stationary biking/spinning | _____ |
| Cycling | _____ |
| Jogging/running | _____ |
| Swimming | _____ |
| Racquetball or squash | _____ |
| Tennis | _____ |
| Dance exercise | _____ |
| Other aerobic activity | _____ |
| Strength training | _____ |
| Stretching/yoga | _____ |

What do you want exercise to do for you? Rate each goal on a scale of 1 to 10
(1 being the least important, 10 being the most important):

| | |
|---|---|
| Improve cardiovascular fitness | _____ |
| Reshape or tone my body | _____ |
| Body-fat/weight loss | _____ |
| Improve performance for a specific sport or activity | _____ |
| Improve mood | _____ |
| Improve ability to cope with stress | _____ |
| Improve flexibility | _____ |
| Increase strength | _____ |
| Increase energy level | _____ |
| Feel better physically overall | _____ |

Other: _____ Please explain: _____

_____

Would you like to change your current weight?  ❒ Yes   ❒ No

If yes, how much would you like to lose?: _____ Gain?: _____

# Medical Screening

Name: _____ Date: _____

Address _____

City: _____ State: _____ Zip: _____

Phone (day): _____ (evening): _____

Height: _____ Weight: _____

Body Mass Index: _____

_____

Blood pressure: _____

_____

Lung function: _____

_____

Body composition: _____

_____

Cardiovascular condition: _____

_____

Flexibility: _____

_____

Strength: _____

_____

# Health History

Name: _____ Date: _____

Address: _____

Phone (day): _____ (evening): _____

Age: _____ Birth date: _____ Gender: ❒ Male  ❒ Female

Are you currently taking any medication?  ❒ Yes   ❒ No

Type: _____ Purpose: _____

Type: _____ Purpose: _____

Type: _____ Purpose: _____

Could any of these medications cause a reaction while exercising?
❒ Yes   ❒ No   If yes, please explain: _____

_____

_____

Do you have or have you ever had any of the following conditions?
If yes, please describe.

| Condition | | | Description of Condition |
|---|---|---|---|
| Heart attack | ❒ Yes | ❒ No | _____ |
| Stroke | ❒ Yes | ❒ No | _____ |
| Chest pain | ❒ Yes | ❒ No | _____ |
| Hypertension | ❒ Yes | ❒ No | _____ |
| Cancer | ❒ Yes | ❒ No | _____ |
| High cholesterol | ❒ Yes | ❒ No | _____ |
| Diabetes | ❒ Yes | ❒ No | _____ |
| Thyroid problems | ❒ Yes | ❒ No | _____ |
| Arthritis | ❒ Yes | ❒ No | _____ |
| Hernia | ❒ Yes | ❒ No | _____ |
| Anemia | ❒ Yes | ❒ No | _____ |
| Obesity | ❒ Yes | ❒ No | _____ |
| Breathing or lung problems | ❒ Yes | ❒ No | _____ |
| Other | ❒ Yes | ❒ No | _____ |

# Health History, continued

Have you ever been injured in any of the following areas? If yes, please describe.

| Body Area | | | Date and Description of Injury |
|---|---|---|---|
| Heart attack | ❑ Yes | ❑ No | _____ |
| Neck | ❑ Yes | ❑ No | _____ |
| Shoulders | ❑ Yes | ❑ No | _____ |
| Arms/hands | ❑ Yes | ❑ No | _____ |
| Abdomen | ❑ Yes | ❑ No | _____ |
| Back | ❑ Yes | ❑ No | _____ |
| Legs/feet | ❑ Yes | ❑ No | _____ |

Are you currently under the care of a physician for any reason?  ❑ Yes   ❑ No
If yes, please explain: _____
_____
_____

Do you know of any physical condition you have that could be aggravated by exercise or exertion?  ❑ Yes   ❑ No
If yes, please explain: _____
_____
_____
_____
_____

Do you smoke?  ❑ Yes   ❑ No   If yes, how much?  _____

Does your doctor know that you are beginning a new exercise program?
❑ Yes   ❑ No

If yes, does he/she approve?   ❑ Yes   ❑ No

If no, is there a reason you have not discussed this with him/her?  ❑ Yes   ❑ No

## Health History, continued

If your doctor does not approve of you beginning a new exercise program, why?

_____

If you have not discussed this with your doctor, why? _____

_____

Have you ever been advised by a health-care professional not to exercise?
❏ Yes   ❏ No   If yes, please explain:

_____

Do you know of any reason why you should not exercise or increase your physical activity?   ❏ Yes   ❏ No

If yes, please explain: _____

_____

Describe any physical activity you do regularly:

**Activity**                                    **Frequency**

_____        _____

_____        _____

_____        _____

**For Women**

Are you pregnant now or have you been pregnant within the last three months?

❏ Yes   ❏ No

Have you experienced menopause or are you having symptoms of menopause?

❏ Yes   ❏ No

The information I have given on this form is, to the best of my knowledge, complete and accurate.

Signature: _____

Printed name: _____

Date: _____

# Informed Consent

*(For exercise testing and fitness program participation)*

I, _____, voluntarily consent to engage in a fitness assessment, including exercise testing, and a personal fitness training program. I understand that the cardiovascular exercise test will involve progressive stages of increasing effort, and that at any time, I may terminate the test for any reason. I understand that during some tests I may be encouraged to work at maximum effort, and that at any time, I may terminate the test for any reason.

The reaction of the cardiovascular system to aerobic or weight-lifting activities cannot always be predicted with complete accuracy. I understand certain physical changes may occur during the exercise testing and during the personal fitness training program. Such changes include abnormal blood pressure, fainting, disorders of the heart rate, and very rare instances of heart attack or cardiac arrest. I understand that every effort will be made to minimize problems by preliminary examination and observation during testing, exercising and any personal training.

Even though I will be observed during the testing and personal fitness training program, I understand that I am responsible for monitoring my own condition at all times during testing, exercise and the personal training program, and should any unusual symptoms occur, I will cease participation and inform the test administrator and/or my personal trainer of the symptoms. Such symptoms could include but are not necessarily limited to: nausea, difficulty in breathing, chest discomfort, and joint or muscle injury.

I also understand that an emergency protocol has been planned. In the event an emergency situation occurs, I am financially responsible for any emergency services that may be necessary.

I agree to assume all risks of the testing, exercise and the personal training program and hereby, for myself, my heirs, personal representatives or assigns, release, indemnify and hold harmless [insert your company name and your name] and their agents and employees from any and all health claims, suits, losses, or causes of action for damages, injury or death, including claims for negligence, arising out of or related to my participation in the fitness assessment, exercise or fitness training program.

I have read the foregoing carefully, and I understand its content and these and other risks that are inherent in a fitness assessment, exercise testing, exercise and personal training. Any questions that may have occurred to me concerning this Informed Consent, Release and Assumption of the Risk have been answered to my

## Informed Consent, continued

satisfaction. My participation in the fitness assessment, testing, exercise and personal training is voluntary and I knowingly assume these risks. I sign this agreement freely and voluntarily, and not under duress or a misrepresentation of facts. If any part of this agreement is held invalid, I agree that the remainder of the agreement shall have full legal effect.

Signature: _____   Date: _____

Witness: _____   Date: _____

# Advertising and Marketing

In Chapter 1, we talked about the tremendous potential market for personal trainers. With that in mind, you might think that just about everyone is a prospective client. While that could be considered technically true, the reality is that if you define your market as "everyone," you'll find it impossible to communicate effectively with anyone. You need to know where your particular prospects are, where they go, where they shop, what they read, who they associate with, what they're interested in, and what will push their buttons.

You also need to recognize that even though people may need what you have to offer, they will not automatically become your clients. At first, clients aren't going to just approach you to train them—you have to go out and get them. But once you get your business built, you'll find that as much as 80 percent of your clients will come through referrals.

We heard this over and over again from the entrepreneurs interviewed for this book. You have to really work hard to get those first few clients, then the rest start flowing in—assuming you're good, of course. So how will you go about getting those first few clients? In this chapter, we're going to discuss the basics of marketing your business, as well as the advertising approaches that worked for the entrepreneurs we interviewed.

# Marketing 101

Marketing consultant Debbie LaChusa, of 10stepmarketing, says the basic principles you'll use in marketing your personal training business are the same as for just about any business. "It's not that difficult," she says. "It's knowing what information you need and where to get it. From my experience, many books and articles make it more complicated than it needs to be." The most important thing to keep in mind about marketing is to "understand that marketing is not an expense. It's not an administrative task that you have to do. It's an investment in your business," says LaChusa. And outside of training itself, it ought to be a function you enjoy. "Of all the necessary things you have to do in a business, marketing is at least a creative one, and you can have fun with it. You can try new things. And if you track them, which I recommend that everybody do, you can find out what's working and what isn't."

In early chapters, you learned how to identify your market. As you put together your marketing strategy, you need to further define your market, your goals, and your relationship to your clients. To do that, keep these questions in mind as you form your marketing plan:

- *Who are your potential customers?* Are they bodybuilders or middle-aged professionals who need help staying and getting in shape? Are they already fit and healthy, or are they recuperating from an injury or illness?
- *How many are there?* Knowing how many potential customers you have will help you determine if you can build a sustainable business.
- *Where are they located?* Is there a substantial market in your local area?

## Research Insight

**D**istress may have a negative impact on the brain. In research reported in 2007 in the journal *Neurology*, experts found that chronic distress can lead to "mild cognitive impairment" in older persons. The research combined the results of two studies, looking at 1,256 people. During 12 years of follow-up, the most distress-prone people were about 40 percent more likely to develop mild cognitive impairment than people who were the least prone to distress.

- *What are they doing in terms of exercise and fitness-related activities now?*
- *What can you offer that they're not getting now and how can you persuade them to do business with you?* In other words, what would be their motivation to contract with you for training, instead of doing whatever it is they're currently doing?
- *Exactly what services are you offering?*
- *How do you compare with your competitors?*
- *What kind of image do you want to project?*

**Beware!** Before you try any marketing idea, take the time upfront to figure out who you're trying to reach and what you want to accomplish. Without a solid plan and sufficient research, you'll just waste your time and money.

The goal of your marketing plan should be to convey to prospective customers your business's existence and the quality of your service. Ideally, you should use a multifaceted approach to marketing your business.

You probably already answered most of these questions when you did your market research. Now it's time to expand on that information and use it to construct a marketing program.

# Getting the Word Out

Personal trainers usually don't spend very much on advertising. In fact, advertising should be a very small part of your overall marketing strategy, but there are times when it's a worthwhile investment. The advertising media you'll want to consider include:

- Word of mouth
- Local television and radio
- Local newspapers
- Direct mail (sales letters, newsletters, fliers, brochures, etc.)

Choosing an advertising medium is particularly challenging for a small operation like a homebased personal training service or even a small studio. Typically, big-city television,

> **Bright Idea**
>
> When you see an ad or other marketing effort being repeated over time, it's a good sign that it's working and you should consider using the same technique for your own company.

radio, and newspapers are too expensive, and magazines are expensive and cover too broad an area to be cost effective. You may find small local newspapers and community publications to be reasonably priced; you'll only know whether or not they'll be effective for you if you try them.

None of the trainers we asked thought a traditional Yellow Pages ad was worthwhile, since they get 80 percent or more of their clients from referrals once they're established.

When evaluating prospective advertising media, consider these factors:

- *Cost per contact.* How much will it cost to reach each prospective customer? For example, if you are buying an ad in a magazine or newspaper, divide the price by the circulation to figure the cost per contact.
- *Frequency.* How frequent should the contacts be? Is a single powerful advertisement preferable to a series of constant small reminders, or vice versa?
- *Impact.* Does the medium appeal to the appropriate senses, such as sight and hearing, in presenting design, color, or sound?
- *Selectivity.* To what degree can the message be restricted to those people who are known to be your most logical prospects?

Think through your advertising decisions carefully, and don't feel pressured to do something unless you're reasonably sure, based on your own assessment (not just the assurances of an ad salesperson), that it will work. Don't advertise in publications that aren't directed at your specific market. And don't buy the expensive four-color brochure when a two-color flier will do.

# Direct Mail

Because of the ability to target well-defined geographical areas, direct mail can be an effective way to promote your personal training business. It also allows you to send a very personalized sales message. However, due to its costs, it is more appropriate for a larger personal training operation than a small, one-person business.

## Dollar Stretcher

Look for noncompeting service providers who are targeting the same market you are and figure out a way to do some cooperative advertising. For example, try doing a joint direct-mail campaign with a massage therapist.

The best methods for direct-mail advertising of a personal training business are personal sales letters and brochures. Use a solo mailer, rather than including your information in a cooperative mailer full of supermarket coupons and the like. People don't select their personal trainer the way they choose barbecue sauce, so the less expensive co-operative mailer can cost you the professional image that you can effectively create through a solo mailer.

A sales letter will allow you to add an effective personal touch. It should be personal, written in an informal style, and selectively directed. You might also want to include a reply card that allows the prospective customer a chance to ask for more information or for you to contact them to arrange a tour of your studio if you have one.

Start your letter with something that will grab the prospect's attention. It might be a description of a special offer or the benefits of personal training. It may flatter the reader: "I know you appreciate the importance of a regular fitness routine for overall health." Another option is to tell a story: "Suzie Smith wanted to wear her mother's wedding gown, but she needed to lose weight and get in shape first."

The body copy of your letter should let the prospect know the exact reason you are writing and what you have to offer. Headlines in letters can be very effective, but if you use one, it should describe the main benefit you are trying to promote. Expand on that point throughout the letter, reiterating that specific benefit as often as you can, using different descriptions so the reader will remember that benefit.

## Research Insight

Not all olive oil is the same—virgin olive oil contains not only heart-friendly monounsaturated fat, but also antioxidants known as polyphenols. Other forms of olive oil are processed at the expense of most of their polyphenols. A 2006 European study of 200 men, reported in the *Annals of Internal Medicine,* compared virgin olive oil, refined olive oil, and a mixture of the two. HDL ("good") cholesterol levels were greatest after three week of using virgin olive oil. In addition, there was a greater decrease in indicators of oxidative stress, which can lead to heart disease.

▲

Any claims you make should be qualified by citing sources or offering endorsements. You should also include what the reader will lose if they don't respond. For example, indicate that you only have a few openings for new clients available, and they are filling up fast. Then close your letter with a repeat of the main benefit and a "call to action," which tells the reader what they should do next, whether it's to return the enclosed reply card, call for an appointment for a tour, come to an open house, or whatever.

You can buy commercial mailing lists (check your local telephone directory under "Mailing Lists"), but you're probably better off building your own mailing list through people you know and referrals.

# Collateral Materials

A good investment of your marketing dollars is in the right collateral materials— that is, your business cards, stationery, and other printed promotional items. Just because you have a computer doesn't mean you can create your own marketing pieces. Most business cards designed by amateurs look like amateurs designed them. A poorly written brochure that does not effectively communicate your message is a waste of money. Newsletters can be a powerful marketing tool for personal trainers, but if yours is hard to read and understand, it's a waste of time and money.

Hire professionals to help you create topnotch collateral materials. Small agencies or freelancers are often willing to work with clients on tight budgets. You may even find a graphic designer or writer willing to work on a trade-out basis. While it's important that your marketing materials be coordinated and professional, never lose sight of the fact that your prospects will ultimately be sold by you, not by a card, brochure, ad, or flier.

# The Real Gold Mine

Most of your clients are going to come from referrals or word-of-mouth advertising. When someone is happy with what you're doing for them, they're going to tell other people.

LaChusa, the marketing consultant, calls it relationship marketing. "It means creating relationships with your existing customers and using those relationships to either get more business out of them, or to get referrals for new clients or new business," she says. "It's taking really good care of the customers you have."

And this just makes sense—when you take care of a client, not only do they physically see results, but they actually feel different. They believe in themselves, they're more confident, and they talk about you to their spouse, to their

> **Smart Tip** Tip...
>
> When passing out your business cards, always give two—one for the person to keep, and one they can pass on to someone else.

## Strictly Confidential

Prospective clients are increasingly likely to ask for references when they are considering hiring you. But your current clients may not want their names and contact information given out to strangers. One way to handle this is by asking current clients to call the individual who is seeking a reference, rather than the other way around. If the prospective client is in the studio, you might consider introducing him to people who are there for their training sessions. You also could obtain testimonial letters from satisfied clients that you can use as a sales and marketing tool.

neighbors, to their friends. Also, by teaching clients and helping them to ultimately be successful on their own, you'll have spokespeople saying positive things about your business in the community. "No matter what your advertising budget is, that's the best form of advertising," Atlanta-area trainer Bill S. says.

Of course, you can expedite this process by taking steps to stimulate referrals. Lynne W., the personal trainer in New York City, takes a very candid and simple approach, letting clients know when she has an opening in her schedule. "I also will put postcards out around the neighborhood where I work," she says. Or you can offer a financial incentive, such as giving clients a discount on their next month's fee if they send a referral and that person becomes a client.

Another way to encourage referrals is to give a gift certificate for a free evaluation and one or two exercise sessions to your clients for them to give to someone else. Do this around a holiday or tie it to some seasonal event to make it stand out. Give it in December with a note that you're happy to help your clients with their holiday shopping, or in the spring with a "Get Ready for Summer" theme.

## Medical Referral Programs

Marketing your services to the medical community can be a challenge, but it can also be extremely lucrative. You'll likely find it difficult to get through to physicians because their office staffs typically act as gatekeepers and will try to block you from making contact. Be persistent and creative; the rewards are worth the effort.

Traditionally, the medical community has had a rather negative view of the fitness industry and is somewhat distrustful of the credibility and quality of the various certifying agencies. However, physicians and other health-care providers have begun actively endorsing fitness as a preventive measure in health care. Presenting yourself and what

▲

you have to offer in a professional, businesslike manner will go a long way toward dissolving the distrust that has existed in the past. Consider offering a few complimentary sessions to show healthcare providers what you can do.

You might try a personalized direct-mail campaign, sending letters to doctors and therapists outlining what you can do for their patients. However, unless the person receiving the letter will recognize your name or has an immediate need for your services, chances are you won't get a response. Personal visits will likely be more effective, but you'll probably find it difficult to get a face-to-face meeting just by dropping in.

> ## Bright Idea
>
> When you have a patient with health problems and you decide to contact their physician before proceeding with a training program, be sure to let that doctor know you will be happy to work with any patients who may benefit from personal training. Put him or her on your mailing list and make them a regular recipient of your marketing efforts.

Because it may be difficult to reach a doctor in his or her office, look for other ways to make contact. Participate in health fairs, make speeches to community organizations, and do volunteer work with groups where you are likely to make contact with health-care providers. If you meet a doctor at a social event, follow up later to let him know about your services. If you have a studio, consider hosting an open house so health-care providers can see what you have to offer.

Remember that medical doctors are not the only health-care professionals who are in a position to refer clients to you. LaChusa suggests researching other health-related businesses such as chiropractors, massage therapists, health-food stores, and supplement retailers as potential referral sources. In addition to chiropractors and massage therapists, one trainer we interviewed says he also networks with a sports psychologist and golf and tennis pros. He also does cross-promotions with nutrition stores and offers a discount to customers of a major HMO. "We're very selective about who we work with," he says. "You want to feel very confident that they're in their professions for the right reasons and that they're qualified, so that the relationship will reflect positively on you."

When you get a referral from a healthcare provider, be sure to send an immediate thank you note and follow up with details of the patient's progress. The more often you put your name in front of a referral source in a positive way, the more referrals you're likely to get.

# Ideas for Promoting Your Business

Teaching people about the importance of fitness and proper exercise programs is part of the service you provide. It's also a great way to market your company. Speak to

## Bright Idea

If you have a studio located in a building surrounded by taller buildings, remember that people are probably looking down at your roof every day. Paint your company name and logo on the roof, and periodically put out a banner with more information or special offers.

local groups (service clubs like Kiwanis and Rotary are always looking for guest speakers); publish your own newsletter; write articles for the local newspaper; let local print, television, and radio journalists know you are available to speak as an expert whenever they are doing stories on fitness and exercise; participate in fitness-related charity events; or host free seminars on fitness. These types of activities position you as an expert on fitness and exercise, and put your name and company in front of hundreds and even thousands of potential clients at a very nominal cost.

The key to making education a successful marketing tool is to give people information that they aren't hearing everywhere else. Be creative with your presentation, and make it different and interesting.

LaChusa calls it "packaging your knowledge." She explains, "There's so much information out there on fitness, and people have a hard time wading through what's accurate and good, and what isn't." She recommends that you take the time to package that information in the form of a newsletter positioned as the one to sift through everything and provide your clients with facts. As we saw in Chapter 5, sending educational e-mails can be very effective in spreading the name and reputation of your business. The idea is to give clients more value than just the hour of training in exchange for their money.

Another angle on using education as a marketing tool is to offer a free booklet on some aspect of fitness in your ads or when you make presentations. The booklet could be something as basic as "How to Choose and Work with a Personal Trainer." When people call for the information, get their name, address, and phone number. After you've sent the report, call and schedule a follow-up consultation.

You could develop a workshop to present to office employees, demonstrating exercises and stretches designed for desk-bound workers. You may or may not earn a fee from the company, but the employees are potential clients.

## Is It Newsworthy?

When you have news, issue a news release to your local media outlets. If the business section

## Smart Tip

PR Newswire is an electronic distribution service through which you can distribute press releases that may get picked up by news sources or web sites. You also can get added to their database of expert sources who are available to the media. For more information, visit www.prnewswire.com.

# Exercise and Depression

**A** 2006 study published in the journal *Medicine and Science in Sports and Exercise* looked at physical activity, depression, and mental well-being. The conclusion was that people with higher levels of cardiorespiratory fitness exhibited fewer depression symptoms, and also scored better on an evaluation of emotional well-being. The benefits for depression and general well-being peaked when participants walked/jogged/ran 11 to 19 miles a week. More exercise didn't confer additional benefits.

of your local paper includes new business announcements, be sure yours gets in there. When you open a new facility or expand your services, issue a news release.

When something happens on a national level that relates to what you do, write up a media advisory with a local spin. Local reporters would much rather be able to interview someone in their own community. For example, let's say researchers at a university announce a new benefit to weight training. You can send a note (either fax or e-mail) to the local paper and radio and television stations repeating the news story and offering to answer additional questions. Your note might read something like: "Researchers at ABC University released the findings of a new study on weight training. I have seen similar results among my clients. If you would like to interview someone local on the benefits and risks of weight training, please call me."

## Give It Away

Offer free initial consultations to all prospective clients. Do a medical history, talk about the client's goals, and explain how you will work with them before you ask them to make a financial commitment to you. This is your opportunity to shine, to set yourself apart from your competition, and to prove yourself before you ask for a fee. The free consultation is like an actor's audition—and you never know what it can lead to, so give each one your very best.

Think about how your free consultation can be a bonus for someone else. For example, visit your local exercise equipment retailers and offer them a few certificates that can be redeemed for a free consultation and one exercise session. Suggest that they give the certificates as a bonus to their customers when a particular sales level is met or exceeded. For example, they might give the certificate (with a face value of $150 or $200) to anyone who spends more than $2,000 on exercise equipment. That person is likely an excellent prospect for you.

> **Bright Idea**
>
> Establish yourself as an expert by writing articles for fitness publications, both print and online, as well as the local publications your target market reads. If you don't have the writing skills and/or the time to compose articles yourself, hire a professional writer who will ghostwrite them for you.

When a prospective client doesn't buy your services after the initial consultation, follow up and find out why. Make it clear that you're not pressuring them to sign up, but rather that you'd genuinely like to know why they didn't so that you can decide if you need to make some changes in your marketing approach or your service package.

# Selling Your Business

To be successful as the owner of a personal training business, you're going to have to be able to sell people on your services. But don't let the word "selling" scare you. Most of the world's top sales professionals will tell you they hate "selling." What they mean is, they hate the vision of the slick, fast-talking character on the used car lot, or the door-to-door peddler who wedges a foot in the door and won't leave until you buy. But that's not selling in the professional sense of the word.

When you sell as a personal trainer, all you're doing is convincing prospective clients that you can help them reach their fitness goals, and that you will do it professionally at a price they are willing to pay. You may be familiar with the sales training phrase "handling objections." That sounds much more frightening than it really is. In most professional sales situations, an "objection" often comes in the form of a question, and whether it's a question or a statement, it is usually a request for more information. For example, a prospective client might say something like, "I don't have a lot of time to exercise." It might sound like an objection or even a rejection, but it's really your clue to explain how efficient the program you'll design will be. Prospects rarely will say no without some sort of an explanation—an objection—that you'll have a chance to overcome.

One of the most difficult parts of a sales call is the close—that is, asking for the commitment and signing the contract—but it shouldn't be. If you've been paying attention, if you identified your prospect's needs and determined that you can satisfy them, then asking the prospect to make that final commitment should be a natural evolution of the sales call.

## Be Prepared

Consumers of personal training services are becoming increasingly savvy. They're likely to have many questions for you before they make

> **Bright Idea**
>
> Never say "no" to a customer. When they ask for something you don't provide, offer them an alternative instead.

a decision to hire you, and you need to be prepared to answer those questions. Here's a sample of the type of questions you're likely to encounter:

- What are your credentials? What certifications do you hold, and where were they issued?
- What is your educational background?
- How do you keep yourself current on the latest information and news about fitness?
- Do you require clients to purchase any special equipment?
- Will you provide referrals from current and previous clients?
- Where do you conduct your training?
- What are your policies regarding missed sessions?
- What are your fees and how do you collect payment?
- Do you offer a free initial consultation and perhaps one or two free sessions to determine if there is a good match with the client's personality and style?

# Assessing Your Results

If your marketing program isn't producing the results you want, figure out why and make appropriate changes. Most of the time, the problem will likely be that you haven't defined your market clearly enough or that you are targeting people who are not qualified clients. If you are not getting any responses, you need to examine your methods. If you are getting responses but they're not turning into clients, ask them why. You may need to work on your presentation, or you may find out that these people either don't need you or can't afford you. In the latter case, consider targeting a different demographic group.

Remember this: Just as you expect prospective clients to ask about your qualifications and credentials, you should also be looking for qualified clients—that is, clients who have a need for your services, coupled with the ability to pay you. This doesn't mean that you need to ask them to complete a credit application during the initial consultation. But you should be able to tell what the chances are that they can afford you when you find out what they do for a living, what their fitness goals are, and what some of their

> **Smart Tip**
> Take before and after pictures, and keep them in your clients' files so that they can see the improvements they're making. With their permission, you can use these photos as a sales tool. Authenticate the timing of the pictures by having your clients hold a copy of that day's newspaper.

# Mark Your Calendar

**P**erhaps the most valuable tool in your marketing kit is the calendar. Plan your promotions at least three months in advance and stick to the plan. This keeps you ahead of the curve and virtually eliminates the "feast or famine" cycle of many businesses. Most businesses tend to market reactively—that is, they market when business drops off, but don't bother when it's good. Referencing your marketing calendar on a daily basis forces you to market proactively and keep your pipeline of new business prospects full.

Take advantage of seasonal promotional opportunities: Christmas, New Year's resolution, and "Shape Up for Summer" promotions are common. Certainly you can use these, but try being more creative, too. Consider a "back-to-school" deal for moms, who will have more time to work out once the kids are away at school all day. If your city has a professional sports team, offer a free session to season ticket holders, either at the beginning or end of the season. Look for lesser-known holidays honoring specific professions—Nurses' Day, for example—and target those folks.

other life issues are. Whatever you do to market your business, make sure every element of your campaign reflects your overall goals and the personality of your operation.

# Fiscal
# Fitness

To be a success in the personal training business, it's not enough for you to be physically fit. Your company needs to be fiscally fit, as well. One of the key indicators of the overall health of your business is its financial status, and it's important that you monitor your financial progress closely. The only way you can do this is to keep good records. In this chapter,

▲

we'll delve into what you need to know about record-keeping and financial statements, as well as pricing your services and billing clients.

# Pricing Your Services

The two primary fee structures you'll use are hourly and flat-fee contract service agreements. While some trainers use one or the other exclusively, most use a combination. It's a good idea to offer a variety of service agreements and hourly rate structures, but not so many that your prospective clients are confused. Keep your fee structures simple, but with sufficient options to suit both your clients' ability to pay and their individual fitness needs.

Finding that perfect rate that isn't too low or too high is a challenge for most personal trainers. If you're going to have a successful, profitable company, you can't price yourself too low. On the other hand, it would be equally unwise to price yourself higher than what your market is willing and able to pay.

Pricing can be tedious and time-consuming, particularly if you don't have a knack for juggling numbers. Especially in the beginning, don't rush through this process. You need to consider a number of factors.

- *Overhead.* This includes the various costs involved in operating your business, such as rent/mortgage, payroll, insurance, taxes, advertising, debt service, utilities, professional services such as accountants and attorneys, telephone, office supplies, etc.

- *Desired income.* How much do you want to be able to take out of the business? Depending on your structure, this would be either your salary or the business's net profit.

- *Capacity.* How much time can you reasonably expect to be working with clients? Another way to think of this is to figure out how many billable hours you'll have. For example, if you're working with clients in their homes, your travel time will likely not be billable, so think about how many hours you can realistically expect to be training. You'll also need to spend time doing administrative tasks; those are not hours you can bill to a client, either.

Calculate your monthly overhead. Some items, such as insurance premiums, may be paid once or twice per year, so you need to prorate those costs and factor them into your figures.

> **Tip...**
>
> **Smart Tip**
>
> Though the assumption is that a personal training session is one hour, it doesn't have to be. You could offer 30-minute sessions; you might also consider a "50-minute hour," such as counselors and massage therapists generally do.

Then add on your desired income or profit. Divide that by the number of billable hours you have in a month, and you have an hourly rate baseline. This number can guide what you charge when working by the hour, and serve as the basis when developing contract packages. If this hourly rate is at or under the going rate in your market, you're in good shape. That will likely be the case if you're working from your home or only part time and have little overhead.

If this hourly rate is overpriced for your market, you have a few options. You can go back and look for ways to reduce your overhead or your desired income. You can look for possible supplemental income opportunities that will allow you to reduce your hourly rate while still meeting your income requirements. For example, you might consider selling a variety of health and fitness products along with training your clients. If you have a studio, you might be able to sublet or rent out a portion of your space to a related health and fitness service provider who is not in direct competition with you. Or, if you can justify the higher rate and there are enough people in your market who will pay it, market yourself based on specialized services and high quality. Take the approach of the popular cosmetics line that admits to costing more, but says its customers are worth it.

Jennifer B., the personal trainer in Brooklyn, bases her fees in large part on how strong the market is and what other trainers are charging. She has steadily increased her fee per session over the years. "It's anywhere from $75 to $175, depending on the situation, and the clients I've had for a longer time pay less because they started a long time ago. The clients I start with now pay a higher rate."

Lynne W., another personal trainer in New York, started out charging the same rate as the staff trainers at the gym she used, but eventually raised her fees. Because she goes to her clients' homes and offices, she factors travel time into her rates.

> **Bright Idea**
> Give yourself a raise. Every year, review your fee structures and, if appropriate, increase what you're charging. Your clients will understand if you give them sufficient notice.

Another option is to not charge by the session, but rather for a monthly package with a minimum of three months, with clients paying in advance at the first of the month. Or consider offering several tiers of pricing. You can have one for one-on-one training with a long-term commitment. You might also develop several packages designed to target less affluent clients who can't afford to see you three times per week for several years. Those packages can be designed to help someone get started, make sure they know how to do the exercises correctly, and monitor them periodically to measure their progress and make adjustments as necessary. It's quite likely that the client who can't afford $200 per week for a year would still be willing to pay $600 for ten visits over a six-month period.

# Payment Methods

An important part of your pricing policy is how clients actually pay you. For example, will they pay by the session on an as-you-go basis? Or by the month in advance? Or by the month in arrears?

Certainly, it would be ideal if everyone paid by the month in advance, but Jennifer B. says, "some people are not comfortable doing that. I have people who pay at the beginning of the month for that month. I have people I invoice at the end of the month, and they pay sometime during the following month."

Something to keep in mind is that payment in advance on a monthly basis makes it easier to enforce your cancellation policy. You will want to consider how clients pay when setting your fee structure.

## Accepting Credit and Debit Cards

The personal trainers we talked with were divided on the issue of accepting debit and credit cards. In general, the small one-person operations did not accept cards, and the owners did not find that to be a problem. Larger operations did accept cards, and owners found it to be an easier way of handling clients on a contract program.

It's much easier now to get merchant status than it has been in the past. Today, merchant status providers are competing aggressively for your business. To get a credit card merchant account, start with your own bank. Also check with various professional associations that offer merchant status as a member benefit. Shop around;

## Research Insight

In a 2005 study, researchers at the University of Miami had weightlifters use varied foot angles in the leg extension exercise, and measured the electrical activity in the quadriceps. The vastus lateralis and vastus medialis showed the highest activation with the toes rotated in, while the rectus femoris (a hip flexor that plays an important role in cycling) peaked with the toes rotated out. This indicates the importance of varying a client's toe angle to promote muscle balance.

this is a competitive industry, and it's worth taking the time to get the best deal.

# Setting Credit Policies

When you extend credit to someone, you are essentially providing an interest-free loan. You wouldn't expect someone to lend you money without getting information from you about where you live and work, and your potential ability to repay. It just makes sense that you would want to get this information from someone you are lending money to. Reputable companies and individuals will not object to providing you with credit information. Be sure you have the client's full name, home and work addresses, telephone numbers, and banking information.

Your credit policy should include a clear collection strategy. Do not ignore overdue bills; the older a bill gets, the less likely it will ever be paid. Be prepared to take action on past-due accounts as soon as they become past due.

# Billing

If you're extending credit to your clients, you need to establish and follow sound billing procedures. Though most of your clients will be individuals, you may have occasion to bill companies for your services. Coordinate your billing system with their accounts payable procedures. Candidly ask what you can do to ensure prompt payment; that may include confirming the correct billing address and finding out what documentation may be required to help them determine the validity of the invoice. Keep in mind that many large companies pay certain types of invoices on certain days of the month. Find out if your customers do that and schedule your invoices to arrive in time for the next payment cycle.

Most computer bookkeeping software programs include basic invoices. See the sample invoice on page 132. If you design your own invoices and statements, be sure they're clear and easy to understand. Detail each item and indicate the amount due in bold with the words "Please pay" in front of the total. A confusing invoice may get set aside for clarification, and your payment will be delayed.

Your invoice should also clearly indicate the terms under which you've extended credit.

**Beware!**
Mail thieves operate even in the nicest of neighborhoods. If you receive checks in the mail, rent a post office box so you know they'll be secure.

# Invoice

## Personal Training Services of Houston
1234 Fort Worth Highway
Houston, TX 01234

Date: _____

Invoice No.: _____     P.O. No.: _____

Terms: _____

| Description | Amount |
|---|---|
| _____ | _____ |
| _____ | _____ |
| _____ | _____ |
| _____ | _____ |
| _____ | _____ |
| _____ | _____ |

**Total**                                                    _____

**Please pay: $**_____     **by**     _____

Introduce a friend to exercise and fitness! Call today for a certificate good for
a free initial consultation and free exercise session: (012) 555-0124.

Terms include the date the invoice is due, any discount for early payment, and additional charges for late payment. For example, terms of "net 30" means the entire amount is due in 30 days; terms of "2–10, net 30" means that the customer can take a 2 percent discount if the invoice is paid in 10 days, but the full amount is due if the invoice is paid in 30 days.

It's also a good idea to specifically state the date the invoice becomes past due to avoid any possible misunderstanding. If you are going to charge a penalty for late payment, be sure your invoice states that it is a late payment or rebilling fee, not a finance charge.

Finally, use your invoice as a marketing tool. Mention any upcoming specials, new services, or other information that may encourage your customers to use more of your services. Add a flier or brochure to the envelope—even though the invoice is going to an existing client; you never know where your brochures will end up.

# Keeping Records

Keeping good records helps you generate the financial statements that tell you exactly where you stand and what you need to do next. There are a number of excellent computer accounting programs on the market to help you with this task, or you can handle the process manually. You might also want to ask your accountant for assistance getting your system of books set up. The key is to do that from the very beginning, and keep your records current and accurate throughout the life of your company.

> **Smart Tip** Tip...
>
> If you have to raise prices, make sure the price increase is reasonable, give your clients notice, and explain why you're doing it. You may lose some clients when you increase your prices, but generally the increased revenue will make up for it.

The key financial statements you need to understand and use regularly are:

- *Profit and loss statement.* This is also called the P&L or the income statement. It illustrates how much your company is making or losing over a designated period—monthly, quarterly, or annually—by subtracting expenses from revenue to arrive at a net result, which is either a profit or a loss. See the Income

# The Taxman Cometh

**B**usinesses are required to pay a wide range of taxes, and there are no exceptions for personal training business owners. Keep good records so you can offset your local, state, and federal income taxes with the expenses of operating your company. If you have employees, you'll be responsible for payroll taxes. If you operate as a corporation, you'll have to pay payroll taxes for yourself; as a sole proprietor, you'll pay self-employment tax. Then there are property taxes, taxes on your equipment and inventory, fees, and taxes to maintain your corporate status, your business license fee (which is really a tax), and other lesser-known taxes. Take the time to review all of your tax liabilities with your accountant.

Statement on page 135 for an idea of what this financial statement looks like for two hypothetical personal training businesses.

- *Balance sheet.* This is a table showing your assets, liabilities, and capital at a specific point. A balance sheet is typically generated monthly, quarterly, or annually when the books are closed.

- *Cash flow statement.* This statement summarizes the operating, investing, and financing activities of your business as they relate to the inflow and outflow of cash. As with the profit and loss statement, a cash flow statement is prepared to reflect a specific accounting period, such as month, quarter, or year.

Successful business owners review these reports regularly, at least monthly, so they always know where they stand and can quickly move to correct minor difficulties before they become major financial problems. Jennifer B. does her bookkeeping weekly and studies her financial statements at the same time. "It's a discipline I keep up on the weekends after the week is finished, and I can track my financial progress that way," she says.

# Ask Before You Need

Just about every growing business experiences economic rough spots and requires financing of some type sooner or later. Plan for the costs of growth and watch for signs of developing problems so you can figure out how to best deal with them before they turn into a major crisis.

Asking for money before you need it is especially important if you're going to be applying for a loan, whether it's from a private individual or a commercial loan source such as your bank. Most lenders are understandably reluctant to extend credit to a business in trouble. So plan your growth and presell your banker on your financial needs. Such foresight demonstrates that you are an astute business owner on top of every situation. Your chances of obtaining the funding you need will improve significantly.

# Income Statement

The income statement (or profit and loss statement) is a simple, straightforward report on your company's cash-generating ability. You can prepare an income statement based on your company's actual performance, or, in the case of a new company, you can prepare a projected income statement as a forecasting and planning tool. This monthly income statement depicts the two hypothetical personal training businesses used for the "Start-Up Expenses" in Chapter 7. One is a homebased business, with 20 to 25 clients; the other is a studio (2,500 square feet) that serves 80 to 100 clients.

|  | Homebased | Studio |
|---|---|---|
| **Monthly Income** | $6,250 | $30,000 |
| **Monthly Expenses** | | |
| Rent | $0 | $1,100 |
| Phone/utilities | 0 | 300 |
| Postage | 8 | 40 |
| Owner/manager salary | 4,000 | 10,000 |
| Payroll/independent contractor commissions | 0 | 10,000 |
| Professional services (legal, accounting) | 40 | 100 |
| Advertising | 0 | 25 |
| Internet service provider | 15 | 125 |
| Office supplies | 20 | 75 |
| Equipment/facility maintenance | 0 | 50 |
| Transportation | 922 | 185 |
| Insurance (including professional liability, general liability, property, casualty, etc.) | 50 | 125 |
| Subscriptions/dues | 20 | 75 |
| Continuing education | 50 | 175 |
| Miscellaneous | 100 | 300 |
| **Total Expenses** | $5,225 | $22,675 |
| **Net Profit (Pre-Tax)** | $1,025 | $7,325 |

# Tales from the
## Trenches

**B**y now, you should know how to get started
and have a good idea of what to do— and not do—in your own
personal training business. But nothing teaches like the voice
of experience. So we asked owners of established personal
training operations to tell us what has contributed to their success. Here's what they had to say.

# Know What Your Clients Know

Beyond keeping up with your own professional education, pay attention to what your clients are learning. Reading professional journals is important, but not enough. You need to also be reading popular publications from the world of magazines, newspapers, and the internet. These are the primary sources of information for most of your clients. They are constantly reporting on new trends in fitness, exercise, and nutrition, and it's not uncommon for their credibility to be questionable. When your clients are exposed to misinformation, they will likely look to you to confirm or refute what they've learned.

# Stay Flexible

We don't mean physically flexible—although certainly that's important, too—but flexible in terms of how you operate and relate to your clients. "This is such a personal business and you're dealing with people one-on-one," says Jennifer B. "Things come up and you need to remain flexible."

Lynne W., a personal trainer in New York City, advises that if you are bending a policy, make sure your client knows it and appreciates it. For example, if someone cancels with less than 24 hours' notice because they're sick and you decide not to charge them, make it clear by saying something like, "You know I have a 24-hour cancellation policy, and technically you should have paid for this session. But I understand that you're sick, so I'm not going to charge you this time." Now that she is a mother, she says, she is more understanding of family emergencies and the needs of children. "However, I still try to stick with the cancellation policy as much as possible," she explains. "After all, this is my income."

# Assign Homework

Make your sessions last longer than the actual time you're together by giving your clients things to do between sessions. "I always give them homework," says Lynne W. "Usually it's just a little exercise or two to do on their own. It might even be simpler than that, like the [client] whose homework assignment was to practice standing with her feet underneath her more instead of having them wider than her hips, and to keep her toes straight instead of turned out—because that's biomechanically better for her body. It might be some basic breathing exercises. I've had [clients] do food diaries or workout journals, and then we talk through what they wrote down in a future session or by e-mail."

# Pick Up After Your Clients

Clients may be careless with their belongings, so be willing to put things like eyeglasses and watches out of harm's way. One of Lynne's clients took her glasses off and

# Tips for Success

○ *Keep your education current.* The fitness industry is full of new information and technology. Commit yourself to constant education to maintain your effectiveness.

○ *Learn from other's mistakes and successes.* Study other personal training services and understand what they did wrong—and right—then use that information in developing your own company.

○ *Network constantly.* Always look for opportunities to let people know what you do. Consider joining professional groups that promote networking and referrals, such as a lead exchange club.

○ *Don't be afraid to charge what you're worth.* Many personal trainers make the mistake of underpricing in the beginning. When you start out too low, it's hard to get your prices up to where they should be.

○ *Pay attention to the business.* Keeping up with what's involved in running a business is challenging, and you may be tempted to let it slide in favor of doing things you enjoy more. But if you don't keep your financial and client records in order and handle the myriad of other tasks involved in running a company, your business is doomed to failure.

○ *Listen actively.* Pay attention to what your clients say—and don't say—with words and body language.

put them on the floor during a session, and Lynne stepped on them. "Luckily, they didn't break," she recalls. "Now, if any client takes their glasses off, I pick them up and put them on a shelf."

## Invest in Education

Knowledge builds confidence, so invest in education—even after you've obtained your initial certifications. What the professional associations offer and require varies depending on the particular certification you have. The organization that issues your certification will let you know what you need to do to keep it current. Beyond that, you need to be reading and studying to stay up-to-date on fitness trends and news. Studying current literature, attending classes, going to conventions and conferences are all investments in your business, not expenses.

## You Are Not Your Client

A very miniscule percentage of your clients will think and act like you do. Don't develop exercise programs that would be effective for you; put together programs that

▲

## Research Insight

**I**f your client owns a pet, she may be gaining a health benefit. Research published in 2002 in *Psychosomatic Medicine* looked at dog and cat owners compared with people who didn't own pets. The pet owners had lower blood pressure, both while resting and under stress (doing math problems and dipping a hand in cold water).

will work for your clients. "The majority of trainers train their clients like they train themselves, and they don't really listen to the client," says one trainer we consulted. "They don't pay attention to the client's body, and quite possibly aren't doing the best for that particular client."

## Maintain a Client Base

One of the most common reason's personal training businesses fail is simply the inability to establish and maintain a steady client base. High client turnover and low client retention rates make it hard to run a profitable business. But be aware that trying to have clients become dependent on you so they'll stick around actually can produce the opposite result. "It sounds strange, but I noticed that the trainers who try to retain their clients by withholding instruction tend to anger clients and lose them quickly," says trainer Annette H. "Those clients tend to come to me. I educate them so that they will be empowered to go on their own when they are ready." A couple sessions before their package is up, she asks if they plan to continue. "If not, I can use those last sessions to prepare them to go on their own. They appreciate this, and often come back a few months later for some more training."

Other causes of losing clients are:

- *Lack of results*. When clients don't see the results they want, or that they believed they were going to get, they lose interest and drop out. If this develops into a pattern, your business will not build the clientele necessary to sustain it.

- *Failing to establish goals*. Along with not getting results, it's a huge mistake when a trainer doesn't find out what a client's goals are and confirm whether they are indeed realistic and achievable. Clients with unrealistic goals are likely to drop out when they realize they aren't going to accomplish what they want.

## Keeping Clients Happy

There are several simple ways to help boost your chances of keeping clients, says trainer Mike H. "Taking the time for the little things," he says, "is what results in retaining long-term clients." Try his suggestions:

○ If a client continues to purchase training packages, show your gratitude by giving them a free hour or a late-cancel option (allowing them one free last-minute cancellation).

○ Call a client on off-training days to see how they feel, how they are eating, or to just say hello.

○ Always be ready, smiling, motivated, and happy to see your clients. "After all," Mike says, "part of our job as a trainer is to set an example."

- *Failing to maintain a sense of commitment.* Certainly clients have more in their lives than their personal fitness goals, but when the trainer is too lax and allows clients to miss sessions regularly, those clients will not make any progress and will eventually drop out.

## Don't Throw It Away

Make sure to maintain a database of contact information on former clients and prospects who went through an initial consultation and didn't sign up. In the future, you very well may want to send them a direct-mail piece and let them know about new services or special packages you're offering, as well as the addition to your staff of new trainers they may be interested in working with.

One trainer we interviewed says not keeping contact information is something he definitely regrets. "Now that I have my own studio, I'd love to send former clients and prospects a direct-mail piece and let them know what we're doing. Not keeping those records was one of my biggest mistakes."

## Decide How Much You're Willing to Work

When you own the company, you can't bill every hour you work because you need to spend time running the operation, as well as training. To ward off burnout, decide in advance how many hours per week you want to work, then create a schedule and stick to it. You may work 12-to-14-hour days, plus weekends in the beginning, but that will get old fast, so don't try to do that for an extended period of time.

# Avoiding Burnout

**A**s a personal trainer, you work hard and as with any career, you risk burnout if you don't take care of yourself. To help keep things in perspective, here are some tips.

○ *Have support.* Make sure you have friends or family who are there for you to talk to. Having a support system is helpful for those times when your work is draining you physically and emotionally.

○ *Don't neglect your own health.* You spend lots of time making sure your clients live healthy lives—just don't get so wrapped up in this pursuit that you don't look after your own well-being. Make time for your own workouts and proper nutrition. Being in good physical condition and eating well give you a foundation to tackle the tough challenges you'll face as a fitness entrepreneur.

○ *Set realistic goals.* Avoid setting goals that are unrealistic or overly idealistic—this can set you up for disappointment.

○ *Have fun.* Don't always do the same old tired routines with your clients. Learn new exercises and training techniques and frequently change their workouts. This will challenge and improve their fitness and keep things interesting for you.

○ *Keep a balance.* Don't let your work consume your every waking hour. Cultivate hobbies and interests aside from work—and consider choosing activities that are lower pressure and not deadline driven to truly give yourself a break.

○ *Watch for signs.* Feeling exhausted by your work may be a sign that you're suffering from burnout. You may also lose enthusiasm for the work and eventually suffer a drop in self-esteem. Consider seeking professional help if your burnout persists.

# Be Your Own Advertisement

Advertise yourself as a personal trainer whenever you are in public by wearing clothing with your company name or logo, or some other indication of what you do. Turning yourself into a walking billboard is an easy, inexpensive way to identify yourself as a personal trainer to everyone you come in contact with. T-shirts are OK, but a sharp polo-style shirt is better.

# Give Gifts that Come Back to You

Most personal trainers use gift-giving occasions to strengthen their relationships with clients, but birthdays, Christmas, and other holidays can also strengthen your business. Jennifer B., the personal trainer in Brooklyn, gives her clients a holiday gift each year—perhaps lotions, herbal products, or something else related to fitness—and includes a certificate for a free session that her client can then give as a gift to someone else. "I get to meet one of their friends who they think can benefit from training. And even if that friend doesn't become a client, they've learned something about themselves, and I've had the opportunity to share my knowledge and information."

# Appendix
# Personal Training Resources

While you are an invaluable resource for your clients, we believe that you, as a trainer, can never have enough of your own resources. Therefore, we present for your consideration a wealth of sources for you to check into, check out, and harness for your own personal information blitz.

These sources are tidbits, ideas to get you started on your research. They are by no means the only sources out there, and they should not be taken as the Ultimate Answer. We have done our research, but businesses do tend to move, change, fold, and expand. As we have repeatedly stressed, do your homework. Get out and start investigating.

But keep in mind that while surfing the Net is like waltzing through a vast library, with a breathtaking array of resources literally at your fingertips, you need to use caution if you're researching health and fitness topics. Always consider the source and watch for financial or other possible biases.

## Consultants and Other Experts

*Robert S. Bernstein, Esq.*, Bernstein Law Firm, P.C., Ste. 2200 Gulf Tower, 707 Grant St., Pittsburgh, PA 15219-1900, (412) 456-8100, fax: (412) 456-8135, e-mail: rbern stein@bernstein law.com

*Vicki L. Helmick, CPA*, 1312 Sterling Oaks Dr., Casselberry, FL 32707-3948, (407) 695-3400, fax: (407) 695-3494, www.accountant-city.com/viki-helmick-cpa

*Debbie LaChusa*, 10stepmarketing, PMB 310, 9625 Mission Gorge Rd., Ste. B2, Santee, CA 92071, (619) 334-8590, fax: (619) 334-8591, www.10stepmarketing.com

*The Sports Management Group, Inc.*, facility safety and risk management consulting, 1205 W. Bessemer Ave., Ste. 223, Greensboro, NC 27408, (336) 272-2071, www.clubsafety.com

*Steve Tharrett*, President of Club Industry Consulting, steve@clubindustryconsulting.com, www.clubindustryconsulting.com

## Credit Card and Other Payment Processing Services

*American Express Merchant Services*, (888) 829-7302, www.americanexpress.com

*Discover Network Card Merchant Services*, (800) 347-6673, www.discovernetwork.com

*MasterCard Merchant Services*, (800) 622-7747, www.mastercard.com

*PayPal*, www.paypal.com

## Equipment, Supplies, and Services

*Creative Health Products, Inc.*, 5148 Saddle Ridge Rd., Plymouth, MI 48170, (800) 742-4478 or (734) 996-5900, fax: (734) 996-4650, www.chponline.com

*Fitness Wholesale*, 895-A Hampshire Rd., Stow, OH 44224, (800) 537-5512 or (330) 929-7227, fax: (800) 232-9348 or (330) 929-7250, www.fitnesswholesale.com

*Perform Better*, exercise equipment, information and seminars for personal trainers, P.O. Box 8090, Cranston, RI 02920-0090, (888) 556-7464, (401) 942-9363 (international), fax: (800) 682-6950, www.performbetter.com

*Sports & Fitness Insurance Corp.*, 212 Key Dr., Ste. A, Madison, MS 39110, (800) 844-0536, fax: (601) 853-6141

*SPRI Products, Inc.*, rubberized resistance exercise products, 1600 Northwind Blvd., Libertyville, IL 60048, (800) 222-7774, www.spriproducts.com

## Fitness Organizations

*Aerobics & Fitness Association of America*, features certification and education, 15250 Ventura Blvd., Suite 200, Sherman Oaks, CA 91403-3297, (800) 446-2322, ext. 215, fax: (818) 788-6301, www.afaa.com

*American College of Sports Medicine*, certification and education, P.O. Box 1440, Indianapolis, IN 46206-1440, (317) 637-9200, fax: (317) 634-7817, www.acsm.org

*American Council on Exercise*, certifications for fitness professionals, as well as public education on the importance of exercise, 4851 Paramount Dr., San Diego, CA 92123, (858) 279-8227 or (888) 825-3636, fax: (858) 279-8064, www.acefitness.com

*The Cooper Institute*, a research organization offering training and certification programs, 12330 Preston Rd., Dallas, TX 75230, (972) 341-3200 or (800) 635-7050, fax: (972) 341-3227, www.cooperinst.org

*IDEA Health & Fitness Association*, a membership organization for health and fitness professionals that features continuing education and resources but does not certify, 10455 Pacific Center Ct., San Diego, CA 92121-4339, (800) 999-4332, fax: (858) 535-8234, www.ideafit.com

*International Fitness Professionals Association*, education and certification programs, 14509 University Point Pl., Tampa, FL 33613, (800) 785-1924 or (813) 979-1925, fax: (813) 979-1978, www.ifpa-fitness.com

*International Health, Racquet & Sportsclub Association*, a member organization for health clubs, 263 Summer St., Boston, MA 02210, (800) 228-4772 or (617) 951-0055, fax: (617) 951-0056, www.ihrsa.org

*International Sports Sciences Association*, offers education and certification programs,1015 Mark Ave., Carpinteria, CA 93103, (800) 892-4772 or (805) 745-8111 (international calls), fax: (805) 884-8119, www.issaonline.com

*National Academy of Sports Medicine*, certifications and continuing education, 26632 Agoura Rd., Calabasas, CA 91302, (800) 460-6276 or (818) 595-1200, fax: (818) 878-9511, www.nasm.org

*National Federation of Professional Trainers*, offers education and certification programs, P.O. Box 4579, Lafayette, IN 47903, (800) 729-6378 or (765) 471-4514 (international calls), fax: (765) 471-7369, www.nfpt.com

*National Strength & Conditioning Association*, certification in the field of strength training and conditioning, 1885 Bob Johnson Dr., Colorado Springs, CO 80906, (719) 632-6722 or (800) 815-6826, fax: (719) 632-6367, www.nsca-lift.org

*Wellcoaches*, certification and education in wellness coaching, 19 Weston Rd., Wellesley, MA 02482, 866-932-6224, www.wellcoach.com

# Health-Related Associations and Government Agencies

*American Cancer Society*, 250 Williams St., Atlanta, GA 30303, (800) ACS-2345, www.cancer.org

*American Diabetes Association*, 1701 North Beauregard St., Alexandria, VA 22311, (800) 342-2383 or (703) 549-1500, www.diabetes.org

*American Heart Association*, 7272 Greenville Ave., Dallas, Texas 75231, (800) 242-8721, www.americanheart.org

*American Stroke Association*, 7272 Greenville Ave., Dallas, Texas 75231, (888) 478-7653, www.strokeassociation.org

*Centers for Disease Control and Prevention*, 1600 Clifton Rd., Atlanta, GA 30333, (800) 311-3435 or (404) 639-3534, www.cdc.gov

*Food and Drug Administration (FDA)*, 5600 Fishers Ln., Rockville, MD 20857-0001, (888) INFO-FDA, www.fda.gov

*IRS*, check your local telephone directory for local offices and phone numbers, www.irs.gov

*National Cancer Institute*, NCI Public Inquiries Office, 6116 Executive Blvd., Room 3036A, Bethesda, MD 20892-8322, (800) 422-6237, www.cancer.gov

*National Diabetes Information Clearinghouse*, 1 Information Way, Bethesda, MD 20892–3560, (800) 860–8747, fax: (703)738–4929, e-mail: ndic@info.niddk.nih.gov, *www.diabetes.niddk.nih.gov*

*U.S. Census Bureau*, 4600 Silver Hill Rd., Washington, DC 20233, (301) 763-4636, www.census.gov

*U.S. Copyright Office*, 101 Independence Ave. SE, Washington, DC 20559-6000, (202) 707-3000, www.loc.gov/copyright

*U.S. Patent and Trademark Office*, Alexandria, VA 22313-1450, (800) 786-9199 or (571) 272-1000, www.uspto.gov

*The Weight-Control Information Network*, 1 WIN Wy., Bethesda, MD 20892-3665, (877) 946-4627 or (202) 828-1025, fax: (202) 828-1028, www.niddk.nih.gov/health/nutrit/win.htm

## Magazines, Books, and Other Publications

*ACE Fitness Matters*, the official publication of the American Council on Exercise, 4851 Paramount Dr., San Diego, CA 92123, (858) 279-8227 or (888) 825-3636, fax: (858) 279-8064, www.acefitness.com

*American College of Sports Medicine*, various free brochures, P.O. Box 1440 Indianapolis, IN 46206-1440, (317) 637-9200, fax: (317) 634-7817, www.acsm.org

*Club Industry's Fitness Business Pro*, a monthly magazine for owners and operators of commercial health and fitness facilities, 9800 Metcalf Ave., Overland Park, KS 66212, (913) 341-1300, www.clubindustry.com

*How to Successfuly Market Your Business in 10 Simple Steps*, by Debbie LaChusa, available through 10stepmarketing, (619) 334-8590, www.10stepmarketing.com

*IDEA Fitness Journal* and *IDEA Trainer Success*, publications produced by IDEA, 10455 Pacific Center Ct., San Diego, CA 92121-4339, (800) 999-4332, fax: (858) 535-8234, www.ideafit.com

*The Obesity Epidemic: A Confidence Crisis Calling for Professional Coaches*, Wellcoaches White Paper, accessible at www.wellcoaches.com/images/whitepaper.pdf

*Strength and Conditioning Journal* and *The Journal of Strength and Conditioning Research*, publications of National Strength & Conditioning Association, 1885 Bob Johnson Dr., Colorado Springs, CO 80906, (719) 632-6722 or (800) 815-6826, fax: (719) 632-6367, www.nsca-lift.org

# Miscellaneous Resources

*Club Industry Show*, (203) 358-9900 or (800) 559-0620, fax: (203) 358-5816, www.club industryshow.com

*Fitness Together*, personal training franchise company, 9092 South Ridgeline Blvd. Ste. A, Highlands Ranch, CO 80129, (303) 663-0880 or (877) 663-0880, fax: (303) 663-1617, information@fitnesstogether.com

*National Organization for Competency Assurance (NOCA)*, an organization that sets quality standards for credentialing organizations, 2025 M St. NW, Suite 800, Washington, DC 20036, (202) 367-1165, fax: (202) 367-2165, www.noca.org

*National Commission for Certifying Agencies*, the accreditation body of NOCA, 2025 M St. NW, Suite 800, Washington, DC 20036, (202) 367-1165, fax: (202) 367-2165, www.noca.org/ncca/ncca.htm

*PR Newswire*, media and PR resources, 810 7th Ave., 32nd floor, New York, NY 10019, (201) 360-6700 or (800) 832-5522

# Performing Rights Organizations

*The American Society of Composers, Authors and Publishers*, One Lincoln Plaza, New York, NY 10023, (212) 621-6000, fax: (212) 724-9064, www.ascap.com

*Broadcast Music, Inc.*, 320 W. 57 St., New York, NY 10019-3790, (212) 586-2000, www.bmi.com

*SESAC*, 55 Music Square E., Nashville, TN 37203, (615) 320-0055, fax: (615) 329-9627, www.sesac.com

# Software and Web-Based
# Tools and Services

*Aspen Information Systems, Inc.*, fitness assessment software, P.O. Box 680031, Houston, TX 77268, (800) 414-0343 or (281) 320-0343, fax: (281) 251-7271, www.aspensoftware.com

*BSDI*, assessment, training and client retention software, Box 357, Califon, NJ 07830, (888) 273-4348 or (908) 832-2691 (international), fax: (909) 832-2670, www.bsdi web.com

*Crosstrainer Software Corp.*, fitness management software, 330 Jasper Hwy., Smiths Falls, ON, Canada, K7A 4S5, (613) 284-1932, fax: (613) 284-1951, www.cross trainer.ca.

*www.godaddy.com*

*Gubb.net*, online list sharing, 758 Beijing Xi Lu, Building 6, #704, Shanghai PRC 200041, contact through Web site at www.gubb.net/public/contact

*Guru.com*, project bidding web site, 5001 Baum Blvd., Suite 760 Pittsburgh, PA 15213, (412) 687-1316, fax: (412) 687-4466, www.guru.com

*Hi-Tech Trainer*, online training tools, 6332 Viola Terrace, Chino Hills, CA 91709, (877)-205-3448, www.hitechtrainer.com and www.hitechwebflexor.com

*Pro Fitness Group, Inc.*, 970) 461-4937, www.profitnessgroup.com

*PumpOne, LLC*, workout creation/online sales, 34 West Ninth St., 2nd Floor, New York, NY 10011, (212) 982-5050, fax: (866) 670-5199, www.youPump.com

*www.register.com*, 800-734-4783

*www.sitesell.com*

*Vesteon Software*, 8739 Bandera Rd. Suite 133–155, San Antonio, TX 78250, (210) 325-8982, www.vesteon-software.com

*Wellcoaches*, 19 Weston Rd., Wellesley, MA 02482, (866) 932-6224, www.well coach.com

# Successful Personal Trainers

*Jennifer Brilliant*, Jennifer Brilliant Yoga and Personal Training, LLC, 732A Carroll St., Brooklyn, NY 11215, (718) 499-7282, e-mail: Jennifer@JenniferBrilliant.com, www.JenniferBrilliant.com

*Louis Coraggio*, Body Architect, (516) 768-0889, info@bodyarch.com, www.bodyarch.com

*Richard T. Cotton*, MA, chief exercise physiologist, MyExercisePlan.com and Executive Wellness Coach, richard@richardcotton.com, (760) 930-4090, www.Strategize Health.com

*Ellen G. Goldman, M.Ed.*, EnerG Coaching, LLC—Fitness & Wellness From the Inside Out, (973) 535-8891, egoldman@wellcoaches.com, www.EnerGcoaching.com

*Mike Hood*, Mike Hood Fitness, 520 Hudson St. Apt 2F, Hoboken, NJ 07030, 646-288-2035, mikehood15@mac.com, www.mikehoodfitness.com

*Annette Hudson*, creator of www.MyFitnessTrainer.com, P.O. Box 731295, Puyallup, WA 98373, info@myfitnesstrainer.com,

*Bill Sonnemaker*, founder and CEO of Catalyst Fitness, 3939 Royal Dr., Ste. 125, Kennesaw, GA 30144, (770) 499-9143, e-mail: bsonnemaker@fitnesscatalyst.com, www.fitnesscatalyst.com

*Lynne Wells*, (917) 929-5920, e-mail: lynne@wellbodyfit.com, www.wellbodyfit.com

# Useful Web Sites

*www.affirmativefitness.com*, an online directory of personal trainers

*www.ars.usda.gov/main/site_main.htm?modecode=12354500*, the USDA's Nutrient Data Laboratory, where you can search for nutrient breakdowns of specific foods

*www.hsph.harvard.edu/nutritionsource*, information from the Department of Nutrition of the Harvard School of Public Health

*www.mayoclinic.com*, the Mayo Clinic's information on diseases and conditions

*www.medlineplus.com*, a medical dictionary and encyclopedia, helpful links to other resources, maintained by the U.S. National Library of Medicine and the National Institutes of Health

*www.mypyramid.gov*, the federal government's site for its food guide pyramid, including an interactive tool that personalizes the pyramid's recommendations

*www.ods.od.nih.gov/index.aspx*, information on supplements from the Office of Dietary Supplements of the National Institutes of Health

*www.pubmed.gov*, a service of the National Library of Medicine and the National Institutes of Health, where you can search a database of thousands of journals for studies on health, diet and exercise—you'll find abstracts plus many free full-text articles

*www.realage.com*, gives you an estimate of your biological age compared to your calendar age

*www.webmd.com*, featuring health news and guides

*www.womenshealth.gov*, covers health topics for women from the U.S. Department of Health & Human Services; the site includes a link to men's health issues at www.womens health.gov/mens

# Glossary

**Behavioral contract**: a written agreement to yourself or another to behave in a prescribed manner.

**Body Mass Index (BMI)**: a relative measure of body weight to body height; for most people this correlates closely with body fat. The number is calculated by dividing weight (in pounds) by height squared (in inches) and then multiplying by 703. A BMI of 30 or more is considered obese by U.S. standards.

**Centers for Disease Control and Prevention (CDC)**: an agency composed of a number of centers, institutes, and offices that aims to promote health and quality of life by preventing and controlling disease, injury, and disability.

**Certification**: the act of attesting that an individual or organization has met a specific set of standards; fitness certifications are established by organizations within the fitness industry.

**CPR**: cardiopulmonary resuscitation.

**Empathy**: understanding another person's point-of-view in a manner that still allows objective reasoning.

**Environmental Protection Agency (EPA)**: a government agency with the mission of protecting human health and safeguarding the natural environment.

**Epidemiology**: the study of distribution and determinants of diseases or other health outcomes in human populations.

**Exercise physiologist**: a scientist who conducts controlled investigations of responses and adaptations to muscular activity using human subjects or animals within a clinical, research, or academic setting; exercise physiologists are degreed and certified in exercise physiology or a related field.

**Exercise prescription**: a physician's recommendation or referral for exercise; the recommended volume of exercise including frequency, intensity, duration, and type of exercise.

**Fitness evaluation**: a series of tests designed to assess cardiovascular fitness, body-fat percentage, flexibility, and muscular strength and endurance.

**Food and Drug Administration (FDA)**: the regulatory agency that is part of the Public Health Service of the U.S. Department of Health and Human Services; responsible for ensuring the safety and wholesomeness of all foods sold in interstate commerce (except meat, poultry, and eggs).

**Food and Nutrition Board (FNB)**: established in 1940 under the National Academy of Sciences to study issues pertaining to the safety and adequacy of the nation's food supply; establish principles and guidelines for adequate nutrition; and render authoritative judgment on the relationships among food intake, nutrition, and health at the request of various agencies.

**General liability insurance**: insurance covering the insured for bodily injury or property damage resulting from general negligence.

**GRAS**: an acronym for "generally recognized as safe."

**Independent contractors**: individuals who conduct business independently on a contract basis and are not employees of an organization or business.

**Informed consent**: voluntary acknowledgment of the purpose, procedures, and specific risks of an activity in which one intends to engage.

**International Food Information Council (IFIC)**: a nonprofit association supported by food, beverage, and agricultural companies to assist the media, educators, health professionals, and scientists to effectively communicate science-based information on health, nutrition, and food safety.

**Kinesiology**: the study of human movement.

**Liability**: legal responsibility.

**Modeling**: the process of learning by observing and imitating others' behavior.

**National Health and Nutrition Examination Survey (NHANES)**: a series of surveys that include information from medical history, physical measurements, biochemical evaluation, physical examination, and dietary intake of population groups within the United States conducted by the U.S. Department of Health and Human Services approximately every five years.

**Nationwide Food Consumption Survey (NFCS)**: a survey conducted by the USDA roughly every ten years that monitors nutrient intake of a cross section of the U.S. public.

**Personalized exercise program**: an individualized exercise program based on the person's fitness evaluation results, and personal fitness and health goals.

**Professional liability insurance**: insurance covering the insured for damages resulting from negligence, errors, or omissions.

**U.S. Department of Agriculture (USDA)**: the government department comprised of numerous agencies charged with different tasks related to agriculture and the food supply.

**Waiver**: voluntary abandonment of a right to file suit; not always legally binding.

**Weight-control Information Network (WIN)**: an information service of the National Institute of Diabetes and Digestive and Kidney Diseases of the National Institutes of Health; assembles and disseminates information on weight control, obesity, and nutritional disorders to health professionals and the general public.

# Index